Employment Workbook

by Jonathan Hussey and Jo Richardson

Published by Bennion Kearny Limited
6 Victory House
64 Trafalgar Road
Birmingham
B13 8BU

www.BennionKearny.com

Cover image: © AirOne

About the Authors

Jonathan Hussey is one of the most exciting innovators of interventions for rehabilitating offenders today. He holds a B.Sc. (Hons) in Psychology from Loughborough University and a B.A. (Hons) in Community Justice Studies from Portsmouth University, as well as being a fully qualified, experienced, and award winning Probation Officer. Jonathan has worked extensively in the Criminal Justice System, but has specialised in leading roles within the Probation Service and Youth Offending Services. Jonathan currently works as a consultant for the Probation Service, and has established a successful training company; Intervention Consultancy (www.reoffending.org.uk).

Jo Richardson joined the Probation Service in 2005, initially within the Employment, Training and Education team before working as a Probation Officer from 2006. She worked within a generic team managing offenders who pose a medium or high risk of serious harm to the public, including those within medium and high security mental health facilities, and of an extensive age range from young adults to elderly offenders. She is also trained as an Aggression Replacement Training (ART) facilitator, delivering this to both male and female offenders. Both her roles within the Probation Service have involved a high level of multi-agency working, including increasing the awareness of other agencies to the role of the Probation Service. Jo holds a BA (Hons) Community Justice, Portsmouth.

Should you, or your organisation, require training on the delivery of these workbooks, then please contact Jonathan Hussey and Jo Richardson at interventioninfo@ymail.com

Table of Contents

This workbook has been developed in conjunction with EQUIP -
a resource for the client to use and keep, on their path to employment. EQUIP
can also be used as a standalone workbook for the more motivated
and able client to complete on their own.

ISBN: 978-0-9570511-7-1

See http://www.bennionkearny.com/Probation-Workbooks.htm for more details

Preface

How do you address an individual who commits a crime due to what they believe is a lack of resources or because of a lack of employment? Do we just tell them what they need to do? That they need to 'get a job'? Or do we help these individuals come to value the contribution they can give to society and the community; to create either a progressive movement or 'light bulb' moment related to the benefits of being employed?

Surely, if we believe people can change, then the latter will facilitate a better sustained change in an offender's behaviour? Helping the practitioner to work with a client in developing this form of confidence and self-belief in their clients' potential is what this workbook sets out to achieve.

The use of language

In the following pages, this workbook will refer to the *facilitator, practitioner* or *tutor*. These terms mean the individual *delivering exercises* to the other person. These terms are interchanged, depending on the context, but they all mean the same thing here.

In turn, the following terms will refer to the person at whom the exercise is directed: *client, participant* and *offender*. Again these terms are interchanged, depending on the context.

The purpose of this workbook

The purpose of this workbook is to give the facilitator an *easy-to-follow structure,* to work from, with the client - to help create a basic toolkit for seeking employment, either through returning to education or simply building a Curriculum Vitae (CV).

In order to do this, the workbook is specifically designed to be a combination of confidence raising and awareness boosting exercises. It also contains practical exercises which produce useful outcomes which help facilitate the search for employment or education.

In our view, by encouraging a conscious recognition of the benefits of the delayed gratification of education and employment, as well as the harm caused by negative behaviours, the motivation to 'change' should build up within the client.

Of course, this workbook does not claim that by completing the exercises the client will definitely have an increased level of motivation to seek employment or a place in education. However, if the facilitator can get the client to see the potential within themselves by using these exercises as tools, this will hopefully act as an additional barrier to future problematic (offending) behaviour or even simply empower the individual to enter into education or employment.

This book focuses on using Cognitive Behavioural work and, as with all Cognitive Behavioural work, the majority of the exercises here are designed to create ambivalence (see section one) within the offender regarding the impact of their problematic behaviour. In this instance, the problematic behaviour is assumed to be any behaviour which is non-beneficial or a barrier to the client being able to enter into education or employment.

Who this workbook is for and the target client base

This workbook can be used on a one-to-one basis or adapted to run with a small group. It should primarily be used by individuals who work with offenders, including professionals in the Probation, Youth Offending Services (YOS) and Prison Service; many of the exercises assume the perceived obstacles of a criminal records and sporadic employment histories. However, other professionals within schools, and drug or alcohol agencies, may also benefit from the information contained in this workbook.

The targeted clients should have, at the very least, a basic level of literacy and prove motivated to discuss their future plans.

The exercises within this workbook are applicable to most offenders and offence types, however there may be examples where the facilitator will need to modify, edit, or simply leave out an exercise. Additionally, care must also be taken to challenge 'inappropriate' answers, with enough time planned for each session to cover this. Inappropriate answers in this instance could be from a client giving an unrealistic career expectation such as 'King of Spain', to wanting to lie on their CV regarding their qualifications.

Always be prepared to challenge inappropriate answers as they arise and always try to ensure that this is undertaken in a motivational style (see section one). So, for example, compare the brief conversations below and consider how they play out in a session:

Non motivational style:

Practitioner: Tell me about what you'd like as a career.

Offender: I want to be Prime Minister.

Practitioner: Well that's an inappropriate comment. What a silly thing to say, we both know that's not going to happen, Stop messing about and wasting time and give me a realistic one.

Offender: No. I want to be in charge of the country and make you do what I say.

Practitioner: Oh stop being silly. You're not about to be my boss any day soon. Can we get back to the task at hand please, and choose a job that you might just get. You know you need to get to the college and get some information on qualifications.

Offender: What's the point? You clearly don't think I'm capable of doing anything of value.

Compared to the motivational method:

Practitioner: Tell me about what you'd like as a career.

Offender: I want to be Prime Minister.

Practitioner: Ok. What makes you choose that as a career path.

Offender: Then I'd be your boss and you'd have to do what I say!

Practitioner: There are easier ways to be my boss! Ok, so from what you've said though, I'm thinking that you'd like a management position?

Offender: Yes, that would be great. I do like this politics lark as well you know. You've always said to me that I can only change laws and stuff if I do it the right way, from the inside out kind of thing.

Practitioner: Have you looked at all at how to get into politics? In turn, what kind of things do you think you'll need to have and do to be able to be a manager?

Offender: I'm not sure… I think that maybe, to be in charge, I'd have to have some experience though?

Practitioner: That does sound likely, doesn't it? What ideas do you have about where we can look for careers advice to get you started?

Offender: Ummm, college?

Practitioner: Great idea! So you're looking for a position where you can work your way up to management eventually and maybe you'd like to look at politics as well? Why don't you drop in to the college on your way home from here?

Offender: Yeah, definitely! I'll let you know next week how I get on.

What this workbook covers

This workbook is divided into two main sections:

Section One

This section covers some of the basic theoretical knowledge needed by the facilitator to undertake the accompanying exercises. It covers in an easy to read and simplistic fashion: What Cognitive Behavioural Therapy (CBT) is, The Cycle of Change, Motivational Interviewing, 'Thinking Errors' and Learning Styles.

Following an exploration into what each element is, we will explain briefly, where possible, how to undertake each skill. It is important to remember that the instructions in this book are a brief overview of how to undertake these skills. Should you require any additional training, then please us at visit www.reoffending.org.uk for our contact details.

Note: Should the facilitator already know these skills, then they can simply begin the exercises.

Caution: Section one is primarily for the practitioner's reference and is not designed to be shared with the offender. In our experience, it is useful for the practitioner to have some background knowledge of the facts around getting into employment with a criminal record, the checks that are undertaken, and the application of the Rehabilitation of Offenders Act (1974). As such, there may be times when it is appropriate to discuss elements contained within section one.

Section Two

Section two covers the workbook exercises themselves. Here we explain exercises that will help the client build up the confidence and skills necessary to progress their career aspirations whatever they may be.

As stated above, the exercises in section two are ideally to be used in sequence. However, where appropriate, the facilitator can use the exercises as standalone tasks depending on the assessed needs of the client.

The exercises within this workbook follow this sequence:

1. **Motivating offenders with no motivation.**

2. **Motivating individuals with some motivation.**

3. **Identifying a career path.**

4. **Setting goals and identifying personal obstacles.**

5. **Overcoming adversity**

6. **CV writing**

7. **Job applications**

8. **Interviews; including practice interviews**

9. **Disclosure of offences; including Rehabilitation of Offenders Act 1974**

10. **Managing rejection**

11. **The final review**

Delivering the Exercises

Prior to each exercise, the facilitator will see **Tutor Notes**. These will give step-by-step guidance on how to run each exercise. The facilitator should read the notes and follow them. The subsequent worksheets for the client follow the Tutor Notes.

Now, regardless of whether the exercises are being delivered as single session, or as a sequential programme, they should always be completed with a simple verbal 'summing-up' of what was covered at the end of each exercise.

Tip: the facilitator should never start a session without thinking carefully about, and planning for, examples of answers that the offender may offer. It may sound obvious but if the facilitator is stumped by a question then the exercise can lose its intended impact. This also helps prepare the facilitator to address potentially inappropriate or anti-social answers.

Lastly, when undertaking the exercise, the facilitator should never be afraid to use a *neutral* example from their own lives as an illustration of the types of answers that the exercise is attempting to draw out from the client. However, these examples should **not** be deeply personal – these exercises are for the client not therapy for the facilitator, nor to place the facilitator at risk.

Note: Unlike our other workbooks within this series (see: www.bennionkearny.com), we do not offer any out-of-work sessions or adapted exercises. This is not because they are not needed, but because the emphasis of this workbook is to enable and prepare the client to enter the employment market. It is less about changing the client's thinking, as with the other workbooks, and more about preparation and information gathering. That is not to say that the client will not change their thinking or be moved to a place of ambivalence – however, this change is something that needs to be supported with other concurrent work.

Education, Training and Employment (ETE) is more about the goal and the benefit of being crime free. Research shows that those offenders who find work are more likely to desist from offending (NACRO, 2005). We would argue that this is not because they lack the time to offend but because employment or education provides a motivation and a desire to be a positive part of society. However, the employment must be meaningful to the offenders to achieve this link. As with any other person, a soulless form of employment which does not utilise the skill set of the employee is demoralising.

We would encourage the facilitator of these exercises to know their client and to present the exercises in an engaging way; be this through discussion or doodling on a flipchart whilst sat on the floor. It is the information collected and collated which is important, not the method in which it is collected.

Section One

Cognitive Behavioural Therapy

This workbook uses the theoretical basis of Cognitive Behavioural Therapy (CBT). Cognitive behaviourism as a whole, and in relation to working with offenders, works towards achieving a sense of personal responsibility within the offender for their behaviour and the resultant consequences (Chui, 2003:68-9). So, if the facilitator can motivate the offender to take responsibility for their behaviour and consider the consequences of their negative actions, then the offender may change their negative behaviours accordingly. But how does CBT enable the facilitator to do this?

CBT in itself is a form of therapy which aims to create an 'ability' in the person to address their problems. Unlike other therapies, it is rooted in the 'now' and looks at how our emotions colour how we approach any given situation. It also helps the client to understand how previous experiences may have shaped our current values and behaviour.

Through CBT, an offender can come to understand their own motives better, and challenge their problematic behaviour; replacing it with more pro social actions. In basic terms, the CBT approach believes that by changing someone's thinking, especially 'flawed' thinking, the resultant behaviour will also change. So, in keeping with the CBT approach, within this workbook, the exercises we propose will help the client consider the implications of their actions by informing their thinking.

The Cycle of Change

The *Cycle of Change* was developed by DiClemente and Prochaska as an aid to assist people in understanding why some people are able to make (and sustain) changes whilst others fail to recognise the need for change. It is also a model that provides a foundation for understanding the stages an individual 'progresses through' when trying to change their behaviour.

The Cycle of Change very simply breaks down the process of change into six areas defined by a person's motivation, and indeed ability, to change (Hussey 2012). We believe that it is critical that the facilitator understands the concept of the Cycle Of

Change because one of the aims of this workbook is to increase the client's internal level of motivation to change by, at the very least, moving them firmly into the *contemplation phase* of this cycle, if not through to the *preparation phase*. So, what are these phases?

Using an offender as an example again, initially, a person may begin in a stage called *pre contemplation*, where there is no recognition of an existing problem. With offenders, this can be seen as a state of denial related to either the offence or the harm it has caused.

Through creating ambivalence towards an offender's current lifestyle, movement can be made towards *contemplation* where a person begins to identify drawbacks to their choices and starts to desire change.

The next stages are *preparation* (also known as *decision*) and *action*. *Preparation* to change and *action* are rather self-explanatory. These phases often occur in quick succession as the motivation brought about by a decision to change behaviour feeds into the actions to alter their behaviour in accordance with their newly desired decision(s). If progress through these stages is achieved, then the person can move forwards to *maintenance* (Fleet and Annison, 2003; Winstone and Hobbs, 2006:262-8).

Note: Should the client conclude in the decision phase that change is too difficult, or 'not worth the effort', then this results in a return to a state of *pre contemplation*.

Assuming that the client is now in a stage of maintenance, there is some debate about the next movement of the client. This debate centres around whether, having made a change, a person remains in the maintenance phase permanently, or whether he/she leaves the cycle when that change becomes internalised or a 'habit'.

As stated in Hussey (2012), for some to remain in the cycle forever is a rather depressing thought and so to aim to practice and perfect a change, to a stage where it is habitual, can be a more encouraging viewpoint.

As mentioned above, the potential to exit the cycle at any stage through a lapse or relapse to old behaviours is always possible. A 'lapse' tends to refer to a momentary slip to previous behaviours, which can subsequently lead to either a return to the cycle or an exit from the cycle via a 'relapse' and the abandonment of change (Winstone and Hobbs, 2006:262-8).

For the visual learners amongst you, here is a diagram of the Cycle of Change:

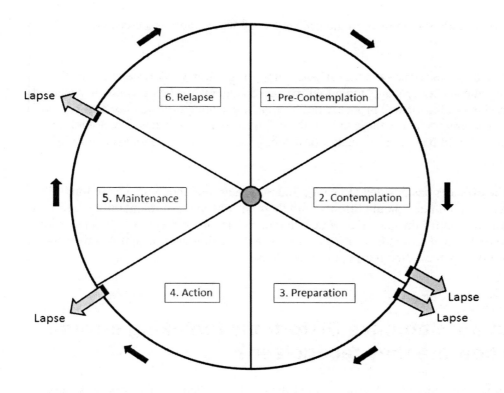

How to use the Cycle of Change

Using an offender who has just been sentenced as an example, and anticipating that the offender who undertakes the exercises is at the beginning of their sentence, we will assume that they are in the pre contemplation stage (with a belief that they do not need to change) regarding their offending behaviour. Here, the practitioner would use their understanding of the Cycle of Change to create ambivalence within the offender concerning offending - in an attempt to move them to the next stage of contemplation. To do this, the practitioner should try to create doubt in the client about the validity and worthwhileness of the offending behaviour. The facilitator should also try to encourage the offender to (at least) entertain the idea that there are other options. This stage can very much be the 'drip drip' approach to eroding seemingly set ideas.

Once an offender has moved into the contemplation stage, where they are open to discussing and even admitting that their offending behaviour is harmful, more work can be undertaken to underpin this theoretical shift; in particular the way the offender views the world towards more concrete behavioural choices and actions. This period can be a very unnerving time for the offender because they are, in many ways, 'undoing' what they thought they knew. So if this happens, and they start to move back to pre contemplation, the facilitator should do their best to support the offender in considering

9

new options and moving them to the decision stage where there is a conscious choice to change.

Note: See how the above says 'assist' and 'support' not *advise*. Advice is a very thorny topic; no one generally wants to be told what to do and even when it is given, accepted and acted upon, then it will probably not be a lasting change as it *was not that person's choice*. The practitioner is there to help the offender make new decisions, not tell them what they should be doing (no matter how tempting this may be) under the guise of 'advice'.

Once the offender has decided to change and puts their new thoughts into action, it is here that the facilitator should discuss with them the obstacles of maintaining their new path. The reason for this is not to be negative or to encourage them to fail, but to allow them to realise and accept how it is going to be a difficult transition and that they should not just give up at the first hurdle, or indeed lapse.

What are Cognitive Distortions ('thinking errors') and how are they recognised?

In order to move offenders forward within the Cycle of Change, this workbook seeks to explore the impact and consequences of the client's behaviour (with the client) on themselves and those around them. The exercises are designed to explore a client's thinking in order to aid a change in behaviour.

However on occasion the client may make a comment which is known as a *cognitive distortion*. But what are cognitive distortions?

In brief, a cognitive distortion is a 'thinking error' (Hussey 2012). It is a particular way of looking at a fact, or part of life, which acts to overemphasise or exaggerate that issue, often leaving no alternative or way back once identified as 'fact'. For example, an offender may have decided that they are 'totally unemployable' and therefore there is 'no point' in even beginning to look at a career or search for work. The fact that very few people are 'totally unemployable', and that nearly everyone has skills that can be used in one job or another is too much detail for the distortion and as such these facts are dismissed by the offender's thinking error.

Sometimes, a cognitive distortion can be a comfortable way of thinking for an offender (or anyone for that matter) even if it is incredibly negative and damaging, because there are no subtleties or unknowns. Therefore change is difficult.

Cognitive distortions do not always lead to offending behaviour and examples of distortions can be found in most aspects of life. However, where distortions related to offending are identified, or an unwillingness to seek employment, they can be key in understanding both why an offender chooses to behave in such a manner, and also how to address that behaviour.

Cognitive distortions are typically associated with depressive thinking and there are many different types of cognitive distortions. Discussion of these is beyond this workbook. Knowledge of them can be gained from further reading and practitioners may find such additional reading useful. Should you want to read more on the types of thinking errors then a useful book in exploring these is the related book (written by one of this workbook's co-authors, Jonathan Hussey) entitled: *Reoffending: a practitioner's guide to addressing offending behaviour in the Criminal Justice System.*

A working example of a cognitive distortion from real life practice could be when an offender tells themselves: "I am a bad person" when, in fact, it is only part of their behaviour which is bad. They may, in fact, be a very pleasant person ninety-nine percent of the time and it is only one percent of the time when their behaviour can be seen as 'bad' or antisocial. This type of thinking error or cognitive distortion is called over-generalising. So, by highlighting the cognitive distortion to the offender, and breaking it down through exercises, the offender is given the opportunity to adjust their thinking and change their behaviour.

When considering the above, it is the internal dialogue which will enable an offender to move through the Cycle of Change and it is therefore envisaged that the practitioner will support employment and education work with other offending behaviour work, as well as more holistic support, concurrently.

What is Motivational Interviewing?

Motivational Interviewing (MI) is a method of working with offenders created by Miller and Rollnick (1991). Where other methods may build a relationship in which change can happen - MI provides a method of progressing and directing that change.

MI is a particular way of facilitating the recognition of problems and addressing them; motivation is a fluctuating state and MI uses a systematic strategy to build internal motivation to tackle them - rather than external pressure (Miller and Rollnick, 1991 cited in Fleet and Annison, 2003:133), linking it to normative compliance. Confrontation is an aim of, rather than a process of, MI (Winstone and Hobbs, 2006:259). However, it is important to note that this confrontation is not code for 'argument' with the offender. The confrontation regards their ideas and statements.

There are five key principles:

1. Being empathetic and accepting of the individual although not the behaviour
2. The development of discrepancies in an offender's cognitive distortions leading to the questioning of beliefs
3. The avoidance of argument through rolling with resistance
4. Seeing resistance as part of an offender's reaction to discomfort with the realisation of their cognitive distortions
5. Supporting efficacy through building belief in the offender's own abilities

(Fleet and Annison, 2003:133-6).

MI is often linked to the Cycle of Change as its principles can be integrated into the cycle. A substantial advantage to MI is that it can be delivered effectively in one session. MI also introduces protective factors which can be considered as reasons to sustain any changes made within a lifestyle. Ideally these protective factors would be internal beliefs rather than external, as the potential for an external factor to change or 'let down' the offender (if it were a person they were changing 'for', for example) can create the potential for lapse (Winstone and Hobbs, 2006:284). It is worth noting, however, that female offenders may pick an external factor such as their child and that this could be linked to social bond theory considerations such that family responsibilities are likely to cause desistance in female offenders (Rex, 1999:374).

As with any approach, there are no guarantees for success; an offender may exit the Cycle of Change by decision if they determine that they are content with their current lifestyle and the process of using MI would need to begin again.

How to do Motivational Interviewing

MI involves being able to direct a conversation with a person so that they are able to discover a truth for themselves. The practitioner needs to be able to read the feedback from the person sat with them in the form of both verbal and non-verbal communication. Listening to what the person is trying to say and reflecting this back to them, either to highlight a discrepancy with their statements or to enable them to find the meaning, are crucial skills. Unhelpful statements are those that contain advice, threats, criticism or direct commands - however tempting.

During any one session, several things are important; being specific in the feedback that is given to the offender (especially praise), listening carefully to the client, using both summarising and reflective listening to prove that the client has been heard, making sure questions are open questions, and encouraging self-motivating questions. These are all evidence that MI is in use.

If the offender resists or is disruptive then change the practice approach, do not attempt to force them to change, this is known as rolling with resistance.

An example discussion using MI:

Practitioner: Thank you for being punctual. I've noticed that you've been on time the last two sessions. Today we're going to start working on the area of employment.

Offender: Urgh – why? I don't want to do some scummy job for no money.

Practitioner: Are you telling me that you're happy with your current life, and for that to stay as it is until you're old?

Offender: That's not what I said.

Practitioner: Explain to me what you meant?

Offender: Everything I've looked at, at the job centre, is just rubbish cleaning or building site skivvy. I don't want that. I want to *do* something with my time and earn proper money. I can't go back to college though so I'm stuck on benefits.

Practitioner: That's a lot of information you just told me. Let's break it down a bit. Why do you think you can't go back to college?

Offender: Well, I got expelled from my last school, so they're hardly going to welcome me with open arms are they...

Practitioner: Do you feel you have changed since that time in your life? And if you do, could you explain that to the college?

Offender: What's the point? They're not going to listen.

Practitioner: Ok. Let's look at another bit you told me before. You said that you wanted to 'do' something. Tell me a bit more about that.

Offender: Well, yeah. I want to work outside, like a park ranger or maybe a zoo keeper – that would be cool!

Practitioner: I agree, that would be cool. The fact that you mentioned college makes me think that you've already looked into those jobs a bit and you know that you might need qualifications?

Offender: Yeah, but I've already said I can't do it. And then there's my criminal record, no one's going to want me with that?

Practitioner: Well, one step at a time. You sound motivated to get a really cool career but you've identified some potential obstacles to that. Let's stick all this down on paper and plan out the next stage for you.

Offender: Ok. It doesn't look like that much to do on paper though, does it?

Practitioner: You're right; sometimes when it's written down it looks far more manageable. It looks like the next step is to enquire with a college about suitable courses; how do you feel about that?

Offender: Alright. Look, I'll give it a go, ok?

What are learning styles? What are the factors to consider for each style?

We do not all learn in the same manner, and learning styles are a way of recognising this. There are three main recognised ways in which we learn:

Auditory: where preference is given to listening to relayed information through lectures or discussions.

Visual: where a person is best able to take in information they can 'see' in the form of presentations, books and diagrams.

Kinaesthetic: where learners prefer to 'do' in order to learn for themselves.

Evidence has shown that offenders tend to be kinaesthetic learners, requiring a participatory approach rather than a didactic one (Hopkinson and Rex, 2003:165) and this is worth bearing in mind when considering the manner in which to deliver an exercise, or whether it needs to be broken down over several sessions. There are various questionnaires available which can be completed with an offender to determine the best style of learning for them. However, caution should be exercised when labelling an offender as having a particular style. It is only a guide and not a necessity to subsequently present all information rigidly in that manner.

This workbook provides a few examples of presenting the same exercise in different styles, however almost any exercise can be adapted. It doesn't have to be a complex process to change information from a diagram to spoken or as an 'experiment'. Below are three ways of presenting the same information regarding an offender's sentence:

Auditory Simply stating: "You were sentenced to three years in custody. You've now served half of that in prison and so been released. You will spend the rest of your

14

sentence on licence. Part of that licence is to report weekly to Probation for supervision where we will undertake work to address issues related to your offending. If you fail to attend these appointments, or break any other conditions of release, such as committing another offence, then you may be recalled to prison."

Visual

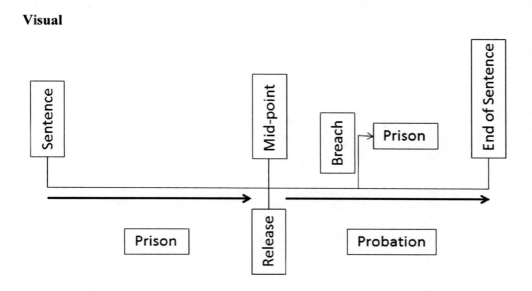

Kinaesthetic Chop the above diagram into pieces and ask the offender to reassemble the diagram (like a jigsaw) with discussion as to why they think pieces go in certain places.

Employment and Offending (optional reading)

The Rehabilitation of Offenders Act 1974 (ROA '74)

This Act relates to the disclosure of offences to employers. It is particularly pertinent where clients feel that their record is holding them back, as they may be over-disclosing their past. Obviously the practitioner must prioritise their duty of care to the public with regard to risk; this Act is not about hiding the truth, but it does allow for offenders to be able to move on and have a second chance. The chart below is the basic and simplified information of the Act and how it relates to 'spent' and 'unspent' convictions. There are some caveats to this chart which are explained below. Note that it is the *sentence* which is relevant to the rehabilitation period *not* the *offence* itself.

Note: It is a criminal offence to fail to disclose relevant convictions when asked. Therefore, if the practitioner is in any way unsure about the application of this Act to their client, they *must* seek help from a more knowledgeable source. NACRO is always a helpful port of call and found at www.nacro.org.uk.

The rehabilitation period is the time until the conviction is 'spent'. Spent convictions do not usually have to be disclosed.

'Spent' and 'Unspent' Convictions Chart

Conviction	Rehabilitation period (if 17 or under when convicted)	Rehabilitation period (if 18 or over when convicted)
Prison sentence of 6 months or less	3.5 years	7 years
Prison sentence of over 6 months but not exceeding 2.5 years (30 months)	5 years	10 years
Borstal	7 years	7 years
Detention Centre	3 years	3 years
Fines, compensation order, action plan and reparation orders	2.5 years	5 years
Probation order, community service, combination order, drug treatment and testing order (DTTO) (prior to Feb 95) Community Rehabilitation Order (CRO), Community Punishment Order (CPO), Community Rehabilitation and Punishment Order (CPRO) (from Feb 95 to Apr 05) Community Orders with Requirements (from Apr 05)	2.5 years	5 years
Absolute Discharge	6 months	6 months
Detention and Training Order of less than 6 months	1 year after the order expires	3.5 years
Detention and Training Order of more than 6 months	1 years after the order expires	5 years
Hospital Order	The longest period of: 5 years or 2 years after the order expires	
Referral Order	Once the order expires	

If an offender reoffends whilst the rehabilitation period of a previous offence is still current, this needs to be taken into account *if* the new offence is one that is tried in a Crown Court. Any offences which remain unspent at the time of the new Crown Court offence will fall under the new rehabilitation period for the new offence. Therefore, it is possible that a client may have a list of minor, summary, offences which will never become spent as they were unspent at the time when that client was convicted for a new offence, and sentenced to over two and a half years in prison.

For example:

In 2000, Brian is convicted of theft and sentenced to a Community Rehabilitation Order or CRO. The rehabilitation period for this is five years and so this offence will be spent in 2005.

However, in 2003, Brian is convicted of Grievous Bodily Harm (GBH) and sentenced to three years imprisonment. Such a sentence means that this conviction will never be considered as 'spent'.

At the time of the conviction for GBH, the rehabilitation period for the theft was still active (the offence was 'unspent') and as such, the theft now comes under the rehabilitation period for the new offence. Therefore, neither offence will ever be spent.

If an offender is sentenced to consecutive prison terms, the total time is the figure to be considered in order to work out the rehabilitation period. However, if the terms are concurrent, then the terms only need to be considered separately.

There will be times when an application forms states that the position being applied for is '*exempt from the Rehabilitation of Offenders Act 1974*'. If this is the case, then it must be made clear on the application form. Instances where this may occur include, but are not limited to, positions which involve working with children or vulnerable adults and those which involve national security. In this event, *all* convictions must be disclosed – even those that would in other circumstances be considered as spent.

Criminal Record Checks

Criminal Record Checks used to be known as 'CRB checks' but are now called 'DBS checks', as they are the responsibility of the Disclosure and Barring Service (DBS). These checks enable a potential employer to request details of a candidate's criminal background in order to establish whether a person is suitable for a particular position. There are different procedures in Scotland and Northern Ireland.

Note: Unless a candidate's previous convictions make that person unsuitable for a position *it is illegal to refuse or withdraw a job offer due to a person's spent offending history.*

It is not possible for an individual to request a DBS check on themselves, however they can apply for a list of unspent convictions; this is known as a 'basic disclosure'. A DBS check will include both spent and unspent convictions and is therefore requested only for certain jobs which are exempt from the Rehabilitation of Offenders Act 1974. There are three levels of DBS check, with increasing scrutiny of offending history, relevant information, and potential inclusion on one of two 'barred' lists. These barred lists relate to suitability for working with children and adults. An employer can only apply for a DBS check at an approved level for the position in question.

Working with a criminal record

It is easy for an offender to feel disillusioned at the prospect and likelihood of achieving employment once they realise that they need to disclose their offending history to an employer. However, a joint study conducted by the Department for Work and Pensions and Ministry of Justice released in 2011 found that between 2000 and 2010, *86% of offenders had been in at least one period of employment.* Whilst there are obvious caveats to this information, including that there are no indications of the length of time of this 'period of employment' or whether the person in question enjoyed their job, the overall picture can be interpreted that gaining employment with a criminal record is not impossible. In fact, given the numbers of people processed by the courts each year, for an employer to refuse to employ anyone with any form of criminal history would severely restrict the workforce pool from which it could recruit.

This is not to say that having a criminal record is not an obstacle in gaining employment, it is. However, it is not an insurmountable one. Offenders should be encouraged to see that their offending is a small part of who they are and that the potential they have to offer remains valid; they may just have to work harder to evidence this.

A research paper by Metcalf, Anderson and Rolfe (2001) found that rejection of potential employees due to convictions was probable in around half of applications, despite the illegality of this. Nonetheless, to turn this statistic around, it means that in half of job applications made, the potential employer is willing to consider an applicant's potential despite the disclosure of an offending history. It is arguable that it may be the wider traits which have led to the person making the decision to offend, such as drug use, which are more off-putting to a potential employer, if these issues have not been addressed, than the offending itself. This is not to say that proportionally offenders as a whole have similar employment levels to the general population – as a group, offenders on probation had an average employment level of 21% compared to 60% of the general public (NACRO 2005). One of the issues identified by NACRO is that offending and

19

unemployment can form a negative cyclical problem for those involved, making escape from the cycle difficult. Simply 'finding a job' is only one part of the puzzle though. For employment to have a positive effect on reoffending, the job must be enjoyable to the person. This is not such an astonishing fact when applied to any other group of people and yet it is one that is regularly overlooked when working with offenders.

The difficulties of obtaining employment with a criminal record should not become entangled with a feeling of being indebted to an employer; gratitude maybe but not beholden to doing something that would not be expected of a person *without* a criminal record. A practitioner is ideally placed to work with an offender to look at career options and paths to this ultimate goal, which may indeed involve lesser paid or less savoury jobs along the way, but are then worth it due to the ultimate goal.

Disclosure of convictions, understanding this issue from an employer's point of view, addressing the obstacles involved and identifying a suitable career are covered in the exercises in section two.

Famous people with records

Whilst there are no doubt celebrities for whom their dubious past has been a selling point, there should be no glamorisation of offending. A crime creates a victim; this simple fact means that someone always suffers from negative behaviour. However, the presence of famous people with convictions is vivid evidence that the perceived barrier of having a criminal record can be overcome. Further, many of these stars have had to conquer the issues related to their offending, as discussed earlier, such as drug use, for example Robert Downey Jnr. Those that do not manage it though are also graphic illustrations of the risks, such as Amy Winehouse. Below are a few examples of notable people who have managed to overcome adversity in spectacular fashion:

Bill Gates: In the 1970, he was arrested three times for driving offences. He is now one of the richest men in the world having founded Microsoft.

Mark Wahlberg: Aged 16 he was in trouble for various assaults, some of which are alleged to have been racially aggravated. He has since built a successful film career and taken responsibility for his offending behaviour.

Nicole Ritchie: In 2003 and 2006 she was arrested for drug related driving offences.

Mahatma Ghandi: Convicted in 1922 for sedition (trouble making), he went on to tour the world protesting and raising awareness about inequality.

Rosa Parks: Convicted of failing to obey segregation laws in the US in 1955 (she refused to leave her seat in the 'whites only' section of a bus), her behaviour/arrest sparked the social unrest which led to the movement for equality in America.

Bibliography and Links

Chui, W. H. (2003) What Works in Reducing Re-Offending: Principles and Programmes. In W. H. Chui and M. Nellis (Eds.) *Moving Probation Forwards: Evidence, Arguments and Practice*. pp56-70, Pearson Longman: Essex

Fleet, F. and Annison, J. (2003) In Support of Effectiveness: Facilitating Participation and Sustaining Change. In W. H. Chui and M. Nellis (Eds.) *Moving Probation Forwards: Evidence, Arguments and Practice*. pp129-143, Pearson Longman: Essex

Hussey, J. (2012) *Reoffending: A practitioners Guide to Working With Offenders and Offending Behaviour in the Criminal Justice System*. Bennion Kearny: Birmingham

Metcalf H., Anderson T. and Rolfe H. (2001) *Barriers to employment for offenders and ex-offenders* (DWP Research Report No 155) Leeds: CDS

Ministry of Justice (2010) *Breaking the Cycle: Effective Punishment, Rehabilitation and Sentencing of Offenders*. HMSO: London

Ministry of Justice and Department for Work and Pensions (2011): *Offending, employment and benefits – emerging findings from the data linkage project* HMSO:London. Retrieved from:
https://www.gov.uk/government/uploads/system/uploads/attachment_data/file/16 2393/offending-employment-benefits-emerging-findings-1111.pdf.pdf

NACRO (2005) *Ex-offenders and employment – the way forwards* Retrieved from: http://www.nacro.org.uk/data/files/ex-offendersemployment-930.pdf (2005)

Rehabilitation of Offenders Act 1974. Retrieved from http://www.justice.gov.uk/downloads/offenders/rehabilitation/rehabilitation-offenders.pdf

Rex, S. (1999) Desistance from Offending: Experiences of Probation, *The Howard Journal*, 38(4), 366-383

Spalek, B. (2003) Victim Work in the Probation Service: Perpetuating Notions of an Ideal Victim. In W.H. Chui and M. Nellis (Eds.) *Moving Probation Forwards. Evidence, Arguments and Practice*. pp.215-225 Pearson Longman: Harlow

Walklate, S. (2004) *Gender, Crime and Criminal Justice (2nd ed.)* Willan: Devon

Winstone, J. and Hobbs, S. (2006) *Strategies for Tackling Offending Behaviour, Volume 2*. 231-395, University of Portsmouth: Portsmouth

https://www.gov.uk/exoffenders-and-employment

https://www.gov.uk/employers-checks-job-applicants

https://www.gov.uk/disclosure-barring-service-check

Section 2

The Exercises

The exercises within this book can be adapted for all variations and levels of required career guidance. Despite our use of the term "offender", as discussed in section one of this workbook, this by no means excludes other users of this workbook. For instance, this workbook is ideal to get a younger person 'going' when they first start to look for work.

The exercises have been written with a target audience of both male and female clients, aged fifteen and older. However, should a practitioner feel that a younger person would benefit from this workbook, care would need to be taken to ensure the language used and examples within exercises are appropriate.

Although this workbook is primarily aimed at supporting a client into work, there are exercises such as 'disclosure of offences' and 'managing rejection' which may bring forwards information regarding more personal experiences or emotions. As such, the facilitator should ensure that they are prepared to support the client in managing such matters before the session is ended.

The following exercises are heavily based on completing worksheets, this is simply due to the sheer volume of information that both the client and practitioner need to assimilate, sort through, and validate for relevance. However, this should not mean that they are less accessible to those with kinaesthetic or auditory learning styles (see section one). Practitioners should consider, before presenting each exercise, whether they would be better to act as the scribe, or ask the client to perform this function; whether the information should be discussed in a less formal manner and recorded on the worksheet by the practitioner afterwards; whether the exercise should be transferred to a flipchart and completed there or indeed whether the flipchart sheet should be torn off the board and laid on the floor to allow the client to move around it. As long as the relevant information is collated, there are no limits on varying the data collection style.

Exercise 1 – Career Direction: "I don't know what I want to do"

Tutor Notes

This exercise is designed to help the client develop some direction, as we acknowledge that there may be occasions when an individual will present to the facilitator as not fully knowing or appreciating their potential. However, if the client does have some idea about what direction they want to go in (education or employment-wise) then it is worthwhile starting at exercise 2.

When undertaking this exercise, there is no need for an offender to 'aim low' because they feel disadvantaged, the only criterion is realism. They may not be able to be a professional footballer at this point, but there are many associated careers in football from groundsman to referee; these can all be explored. Starting with an area of interest is what will garner the motivation from the client to put the plans into action. It is the practitioner's role to help the client see and understand the concept of delayed gratification. This being that the low paid role the client needs to undertake now is 'worth it', not because of the immediate rewards but because it is part of the 'master plan' to enable them to be, and achieve, what they really want.

Depending on the needs of the client, if starting at this point (lack of direction), it may be better to plan to complete this exercise over several sessions.

Caution: When working with offenders, the practitioner *must* check previous convictions *first* to ensure that the offender is not barred from working with particular groups, or simply unsuitable for an area of work (for example, some serious violent offences would bar a person from working as a doorman as they would not be able to gain Security Industry Authority (SIA) approval. Similarly, a sex offender would not be able to work with children).

Tip: If you are not working in the Criminal Justice System but know you are working with an offender, you can ask the client to give written consent so that you can approach, where applicable, their Probation Officer to find out their previous convictions.

Step 1: Using worksheet 1, ask the client to complete the picture by adding their attributes around the outside of the figure. These attributes can be anything that the client can think of about themselves, both physical and non-visible. Allow any answer at this stage; 'being strong' could be useful for employment if the client decides to be a builder, for example.

Tip: If the client struggles to think of answers, prompt them with both examples but also by asking them what people tend to compliment them on. For example, good manners or being punctual.

Step 2: Ask the client to sort the attributes into the table at the bottom of the worksheet. They need to look for attributes which could be useful in employment and then *why* they may be useful.

Tip: The answers given in the 'why' section should start to give an idea of the areas of interest of the client. For instance, if they decide that 'good manners' would be useful because 'I can talk to customers', then they may be thinking of people-orientated posts and working in a team.

Step 3: Move to worksheet 2. Using a highlighter, ask the client to mark as many of the points that are relevant to them as possible. The client can add their own ideas here, too.

Step 4: Using a brainstorming style of exercise, ask the client to consider all of the aspects and areas of life that interest them. Anything *legal* is applicable here. Once they have finished, ask them to rank the highlighted points from step 3 and their brainstorming points in order to create a 'top 10'.

Step 5: On worksheet 3, using information from worksheets 1 and 2, the client should now be able to complete the statements to make a cohesive statement regarding what they are looking for in terms of a career.

Exercise 1 – Worksheet 1

Complete the diagram by adding all the attributes you can think of about yourself:

Attributes that could be useful in employment	Why…?

Exercise 1 – Worksheet 2

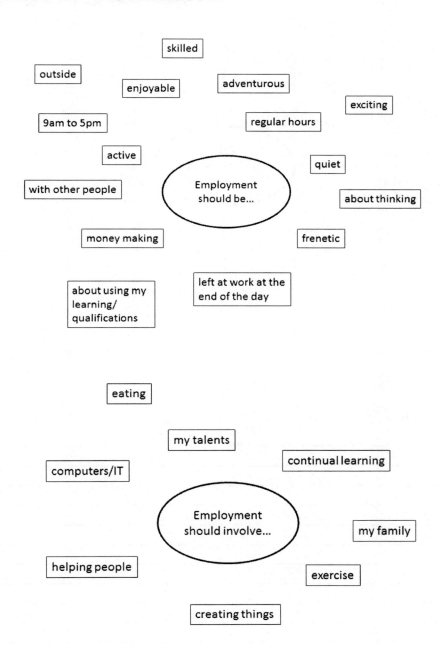

skilled

outside

enjoyable

adventurous

exciting

9am to 5pm

regular hours

active

quiet

with other people

Employment should be...

about thinking

money making

frenetic

about using my learning/ qualifications

left at work at the end of the day

eating

my talents

continual learning

computers/IT

Employment should involve...

my family

helping people

exercise

creating things

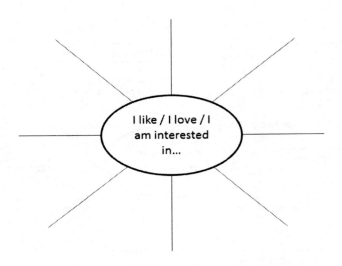

I like / I love / I am interested in...

My Top Ten list

1	
2	
3	
4	
5	
6	
7	
8	
9	
10	

Exercise 1 – Worksheet 3

For my career, I would like a job that involves:

-
-
-
-
-

The job itself should be:

-
-
-
-
-

I believe that I have the following qualities:

-
-
-
-
-

And these qualities will be useful because:

_____

_____

_____

If you now have any ideas regarding possible careers or jobs, note them here:

_____

_____

_____

Exercise 1 – Review

Name at least one thing that has been learned from this exercise.

Additional Notes:

Exercise 2 – Motivation and Direction: "I have a rough idea of what I want to do"

Tutor Notes

When working with clients, some may have some idea as to whether they want to get involved with education, or begin work in a broad area. The only problem being that the client does not have a specific path to follow and stays 'stuck' where they are. This exercise attempts to resolve this conflict and promote some direction.

Step 1: Using worksheet 1, complete the top box of the flowchart with an area that the client is interested in. This can be a wide ranging and general area, or a more pinpointed one. The exercise will work with either.

Note: If the client has completed exercise 1, this area of interest will come from the results of worksheet 3 from that exercise. The practitioner may need to guide or provide direction as to what areas cover those results.

Step 2: Using a brainstorming style, expand the area into all of the related roles, positions, and jobs that can be associated with that area.

Tip: If you are able to take an internet enabled laptop into client sessions, it will be very helpful in researching related jobs.

Step 3: Filter the answers from step 2 through a 'possible' filter to the next layer of the flow chart.

Step 4: Filter again the answers from step 3 through an 'interested/interesting' filter to the final layer of the chart.

For example:

Area of interest – dinosaurs

Related roles – palaeontologist, researcher, history teacher, museum worker, model maker, time traveller, DNA breeder, fiction writer, archaeologist, painter, children's story teller, scientist, cleaner

Possible filter – researcher, museum worker, model maker, painter, story teller

Interested filter – museum worker, model maker

Exercise 2 – Worksheet 1

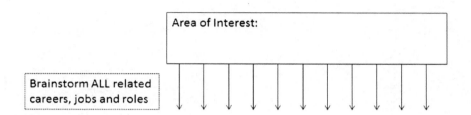

Area of Interest:

Brainstorm ALL related careers, jobs and roles

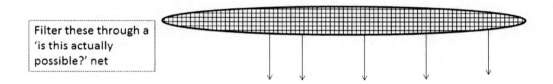

Filter these through a 'is this actually possible?' net

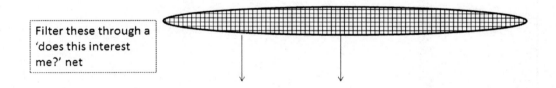

Filter these through a 'does this interest me?' net

Possible careers I would like to find out more about are:

-
-

Exercise 2 – Review

Name at least one thing that has been learned from this exercise.

Additional Notes:

Exercise 3 – Career Identified: "I know what I want to do"

Tutor Notes
This session is ideally used when the client recognises or has a relatively good idea of the career they would like to pursue. The following exercise is about ordering thoughts and creating a 'to do' list to achieve their goals and desired outcomes.

Step 1: Ask the client to think about getting into their chosen field of employment. Then ask them to write down, or dictate, all the facts they already know onto worksheet 1.

Step 2: Looking at the facts, sort out and circle the ones that are related to *getting a job*. It may be good that the client knows the average wage but it would be far more useful for them to know what qualifications are required.

Step 3: Answer as many of the questions as possible on the worksheet. Any unanswered questions should be transferred to the 'what do I need to find out?' table (where relevant).

Step 4: Add any further details to the table regarding information that needs to be sought. Then complete the table with 'where to go to find the information', such as the internet, careers advice agency, governing body for the career in mind, and so on.

Tip: Although it may be tempting as the practitioner to take over this exercise and provide much of the information, the client is far more likely to actually take the steps required outside the session if they have put most of the thought into it (see cycle of change, section one). It may be appropriate to suggest and hint at some answers but it may also be more useful in the long run to allow the client to try for themselves and then review progress at the next session.

Step 5: Turn the table into a list of goals which need to be achieved, in the order they need to be achieved in. Agree a timescale when these goals will be reviewed.

Note: Of the goals here, actually 'getting a job' *should not* be one of them. This goal setting exercise is about finding the information to enable successful job hunting.

Step 6: At the agreed date, review the table and revise the goal setting accordingly. Reassure the client that if, having done all the research, they change their minds - this work was not a waste of time. They have made an educated decision and can simply go back to stage 1 and look for new ideas.

Exercise 3 – Worksheet 1

My chosen career/area is:

What do you already know about your chosen career?

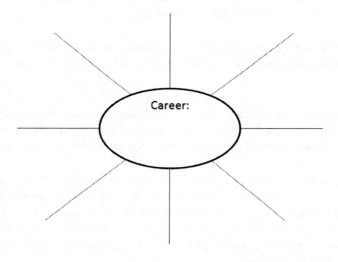

Career:

Answer these questions:

What qualifications do I need?

Do I need to return to college/university?

Where is the most local company/position providing this career?

What experience do I need? What level of literacy and numeracy is required?

Are there any apprenticeships available?

Where can I go to speak to someone for more detailed advice?

Is there any cost involved in getting this career?

Is there any funding available for this career?

Is there a governing body for this career?

Are there any organisations that I should join to help in gaining a position?

Can I do voluntary work in this field?

What do I now need to find out?

Question	Possible source of information	Answer

Agreed date to complete this by:

_____

Exercise 3 – Review

Name at least one thing that has been learned from this exercise.

Additional Notes:

Exercise 4 – Setting Goals and Identifying Obstacles

Tutor Notes

This exercise is in two parts; the first looks at what the client wants to achieve and the steps needed to get there, the second part looks at potential obstacles and, crucially, how they may be overcome.

The practitioner is ideally placed to encourage a client to plan for their goals, to be realistic about steps and timescales for these steps, and to support them through examining the obstacles. A client needs to be able to see that identifying obstacles is not about pessimism but is a normal part of planning for the future.

This exercise is divided into two parts to allow the practitioner to plan for sessions as required by the client; it may be that this exercise covers more than one session.

Part 1

Step 1: If the client has a firm idea of their end goal, and the career they would like to pursue, then write this in the top box. If the client is not able to give a definite statement regarding their end goal then it may be that they would benefit from completing exercise 1 (if not completing the exercises sequentially).

Step 2: A worksheet is provided but given the volume of information collated at this stage, it may be best practice to use an A1 flipchart sheet. Go through the numbered questions on worksheet 1 with the client in sequential order. Where the client answers 'yes' then this needs to be added as a step towards the end goal. The questions are closed questions and it is the '*how*' which the box will eventually evidence (after step 3). So for example, question 1 is – do you need experience? If the client says yes *and they do not have or cannot evidence this experience* then 'get experience' would be the first step.

Note: If the answer to a question is 'yes' but the client has already achieved this step, then it can sometimes be motivational to add it to the stepping stones anyway, so that they can see how far they have come already.

Step 3: The box for each step now needs to be turned into a brainstorming box. So using the above example 'get experience', it needs to be brainstormed with the client how this would be achieved. The most suitable and likely suggestion should then be highlighted.

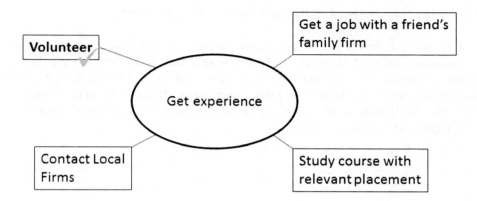

Step 4: Rewrite the chain (with just the step and most likely solution for that step (the answers to steps 2 and 3) so that there are clear stepping stones of smaller goals to be achieved towards the end goal.

Note: Keep the original brainstormed stepping stones so that if any of the chosen likely solutions are later deemed to be non-viable, then the original can be referred to again for new ideas.

Part 2

Step 1: Ask the client to think of any obstacles 'off the top of their head'; this will give the practitioner an idea of the problem which is foremost in the client's mind. Write this on worksheet 4.

Step 2: Looking at the stepping stones they have identified in stage 1, take each stone individually and discuss if there are any obvious obstacles, then write these on worksheet 4.

Step 3: Complete worksheet 3 with the client. Match the obstacles in the no entry signs to potential strategies in the ticks – there are no 'correct' answers here. The practitioner should look to encourage discussion. For kinaesthetic learners, it would be appropriate to ask the client to actually draw lines to connect the problems with solutions. Transfer any relevant answers to the questions at the foot of the page to worksheet 4.

Step 4: Complete worksheet 4 with the client. Allow the client to lead as much as possible so that the possible strategies or diversions are their idea (remember: MI style of working) but guide so that the solutions are viable.

Step 5: Merge the completed worksheets 2 and 4 onto worksheet 5.

Note: As previously mentioned in section one, these exercises have a tendency to be heavily worksheet reliant. If, as a practitioner, your assessment of the client is that this will have an adverse effect then change the presentation style of the exercise and record the information on the worksheet yourself. For example; brainstorm onto a flipchart sheet, or physically walk on the 'stepping stones' having written the small steps on a piece of paper and discuss the obstacles.

Exercise 4 – Worksheet 1

1. Do you need experience?

2. Do you have the relevant literacy and numeracy level?

3. Do you need qualifications?

4. Would it be useful to contact local colleges/adult learning facilities?

5. Would it be helpful to find a suitable voluntary post?

6. Would it be helpful to find a related (but potentially lower paid) position? For example, getting an administrative post in the same company you wish to be a lawyer.

7. Would it be helpful to contact all the relevant local companies for advice/support?

8. Do you have an up-to-date CV?

9. Would it be helpful to send out your CV to relevant firms?

10. Is there a relevant governing body or organisation that it would be helpful to join?

11. Are there any licences, such as a driving licence, which is required for the end goal?

12. Are there any negative cost implications to undertaking the previous steps? (How will you overcome this?)

Exercise 4 – Worksheet 2

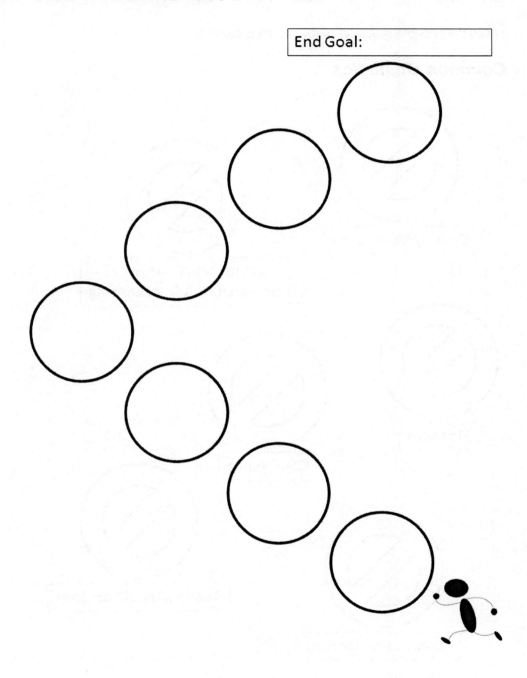

End Goal:

Exercise 4 – Worksheet 3

Match the possible strategies to the common problems.

Common Obstacles

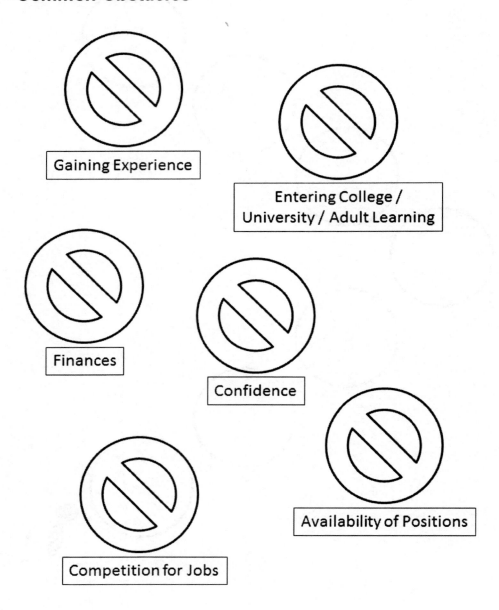

Gaining Experience

Entering College /
University / Adult Learning

Finances

Confidence

Competition for Jobs

Availability of Positions

Useful Strategies

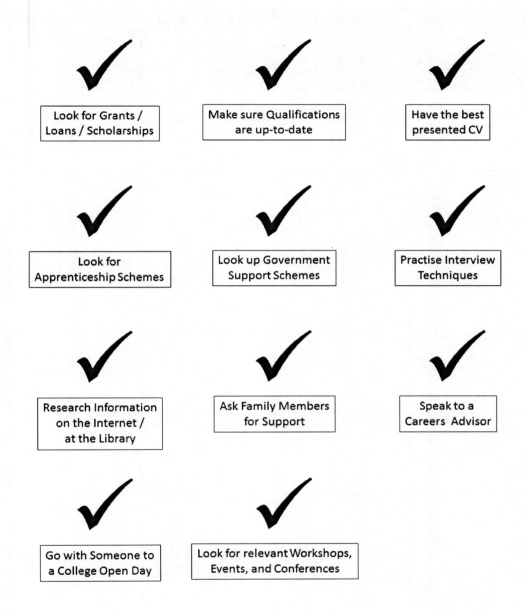

Look for Grants / Loans / Scholarships

Make sure Qualifications are up-to-date

Have the best presented CV

Look for Apprenticeship Schemes

Look up Government Support Schemes

Practise Interview Techniques

Research Information on the Internet / at the Library

Ask Family Members for Support

Speak to a Careers Advisor

Go with Someone to a College Open Day

Look for relevant Workshops, Events, and Conferences

Do any of the common problems apply to you? Which strategies may also apply?

Exercise 4 – Worksheet 4

Identified obstacles	Possible strategies	Most likely strategy	When do I need to do this for/by?

Exercise 4 – Worksheet 5

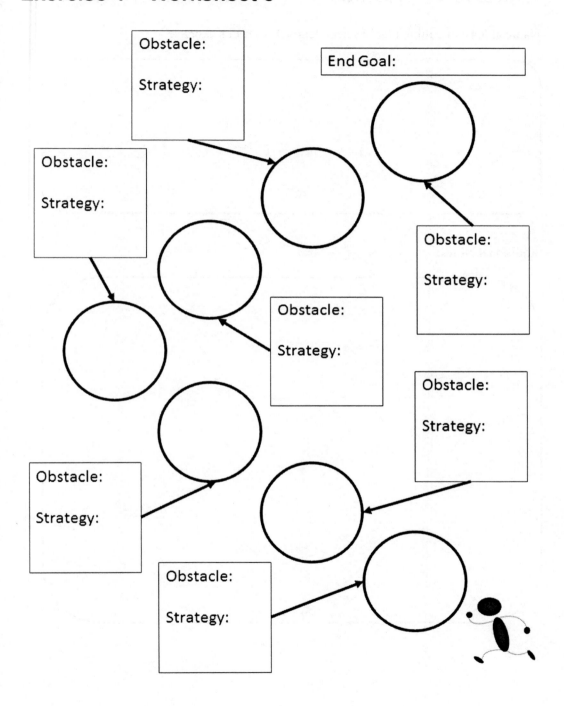

Exercise 4 – Review

Name at least one thing that has been learned from this exercise.

Additional Notes:

Exercise 5 – Overcoming Adversity

Tutor Notes

Some clients may feel that achieving their goal is impossible. It is all too easy to look around at people who have 'made it' and forget that they did not simply wake up one morning and bump in to their success at the front door without an awful lot of effort. It is also important to remember that 'failure' is both normal and to be expected on some level – for every time something goes right, it has probably previously gone a little bit astray too. There is no need to give up at the first hurdle.

As with the strategies identified in exercise 4 to overcome the client's own obstacles, the well-known people in this exercise will have had to plan and prepare their own strategies. Many clients may retort that 'it's alright for them, they have money,' but the people on worksheet 1 did not always have money. In some cases, money would have made little difference and the biggest hurdles may have been overcome at times of financial difficulty. The one thing the people in this exercise have in common is that although they may have felt rejected or discouraged, they didn't give up.

Note: This exercise is not about telling every client that they can also be rich and famous. These people are usually the exceptions. However, the overall message should be that we can achieve our goals if we simply believe in ourselves and keep working towards them *in the face* of obstacles.

Step 1: On worksheet 1, read through the list of people with the client and make sure that they know who the people are. Look at the sections of achievements and obstacles which were overcome and ask the client to match each of the people with these. For more kinaesthetic learners, cut out the names and statements and ask the client to group the relevant person, obstacle, and achievement together on the table; or ask the client to join the answers together by using different colours for each person.

Steps 2: Move to worksheet 2. Discuss with the client a person (famous, family, or friend) who they feel has personally inspired them, or who is inspirational to them, at any point in their life so far. Write the relevant person at the top and, with the client, break down *why* it is that they feel this person was an inspiration.

Step 3: The second part of worksheet 2 is for the client to consider someone that they would like to think finds *them* inspirational. Write down what achievement they would like to be admired for; what do they want the person to 'see' when they look at them? Also note what obstacles they have/will tackle and *how*.

Answers to Worksheet 1

Stevie Wonder (singer)

Blind from birth.

Won 22 Grammy awards over his 51 year career and has had numerous number 1 hits in the US and UK.

Jim Carrey (actor/comedian)

Experienced poverty as a child, had to live with his family in a van for a time and worked an 8 hour shift after school to help his family make ends meet. Has ADHD.

Renowned multi-million pound earning actor.

Richard Branson (CEO Virgin)

Dyslexic and discouraged as a child from believing he could achieve. Had some high profile failures as a businessman including a cola brand and credit card.

Chief Executive of his own company, regularly in the top 5 of the UK rich list and owns his own Caribbean island.

Albert Einstein (scientist)

Didn't speak as a child until aged 4 and didn't read until aged 7. Failed his college entrance exam.

Considered the 'father' of modern physics, published numerous ground-breaking papers, and is well known for his equation $E=MC^2$.

Angelina Jolie (actress)

Suffered suicidal thoughts and depression as a child, and used self-harming as a coping strategy. Required pre-emptive surgery for cancer scare as an adult.

Humanitarian Ambassador for the UN, multi-million pound and award winning actress.

Stephen Spielberg (director)

Rejected from a film and theatre college three times then, when eventually accepted, dropped out before completing the course to take up a job.

Director of many blockbuster films.

JK Rowling (author)

Book manuscript rejected by 12 publishers and even when accepted by a publisher, told there would be no money in it.

Author of the phenomenally popular Harry Potter novels.

The Beatles (musicians)

Rejected by record labels as being outdated and having 'no future' in the industry.

Major band in the 1960s.

Exercise 5 – Worksheet 1

Personality

Stevie Wonder   **Jim Carrey**   **Richard Branson**

Albert Einstein   **Angelina Jolie**

Stephen Spielberg   **JK Rowling**   **The Beatles**

Obstacle

Book manuscript rejected by 12 publishers and even when accepted by a publisher, told there would be no money in it.

Blind from birth.

Didn't speak as a child until aged 4 and didn't read until aged 7.
Failed his college entrance exam.

Experienced poverty as a child, had to live with his family in a van for a time and worked an 8 hour shift after school to help his family make ends meet.
Has ADHD.

Rejected by record labels as being outdated and having 'no future' in the industry.

Suffered suicidal thoughts and depression as a child, and used self-harming as a coping strategy. Required pre-emptive surgery for cancer scare as an adult.

Rejected from a film and theatre college three times then, when eventually accepted, dropped out before completing the course to take up a job.

Dyslexic and discouraged as a child from believing he could achieve. Had some high profile failures as a businessman including a cola brand and credit card.

Achievement

Won 22 Grammy awards over his 51 year career and has had numerous number 1 hits in the US and UK.

Humanitarian Ambassador for the UN, multi-million pound and award winning actress.

Major band in the 1960s.

Renowned multi-million pound earning actor.

Considered the 'father' of modern physics, published numerous ground-breaking papers, and is well known for his equation $E=MC^2$.

Author of the phenomenally popular Harry Potter novels.

Chief Executive of his own company, regularly in the top 5 of the
UK rich list and owns his own Caribbean island.

Director of many blockbuster films.

Exercise 5 – Worksheet 2

Name a person that you find inspirational.

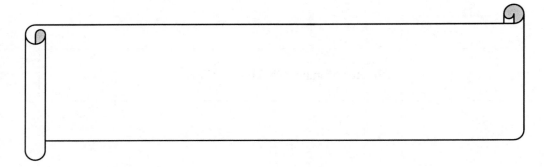

What have they done or achieved to make you think of them as inspirational?

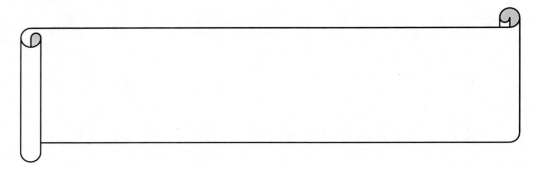

What obstacles have they overcome in order to achieve their goal?

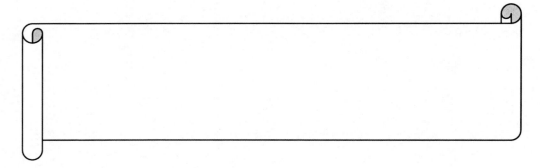

Think of someone that you would like to admire you, and even consider you as an inspiration to them.

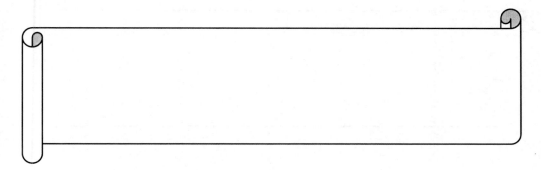

What would you like to achieve in order to be an inspiration?

What obstacles do you need to overcome in order to do this?

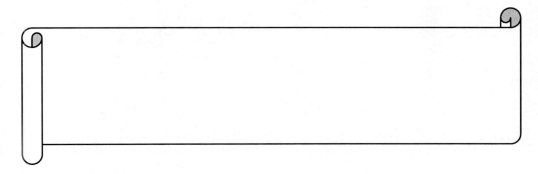

How will you do this?

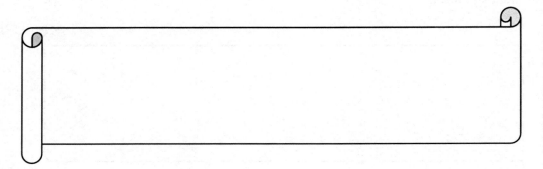

Exercise 5 – Review

Name at least one thing that has been learned from this exercise.

Additional Notes:

Exercise 6 – CV Writing

Tutor Notes

Everyone and every industry has their own opinion on the 'correct' format for a CV. The truth is that there is no definitive format and the presentation will remain a very personal thing. However, there are certain pieces of information which are usually required (or not required), common guidelines, and ways of presenting information in order. These are explored in this exercise.

Sometimes the easiest way to answer a question as to whether a piece of information needs to go into a CV is to look at the CV *as the potential employer* and consider whether it actually tells you anything about the person that would make you want to employ them.

As stated earlier, every industry will look for different factors in a CV and these need to be considered so that the CV feels personalised for both the client and the target group. For example, if the client is looking for a job in the ICT sector, then the CV needs to reflect good IT skills; if they are looking for an administrative post then the formatting, spelling and grammar are going to be of increased importance.

There are three worksheets for this exercise. The first is designed so that the client can take it away for future reference after the session. The second is simply a way of collecting all the necessary information for a CV, and the third contains examples and suggestions for different presentation styles.

Tip: The practitioner needs to consider whether the literacy skills of the client mean that it would be beneficial for the practitioner to type up the CV between sessions, or whether taking a laptop into the session for the client to use would be helpful.

Worksheet 1 – Big no nos, common problems and suggested solutions

Worksheet 2 – Collecting the information

Worksheet 3 – Different presentation ideas

Step 1: Read through worksheet 1 and discuss with the client their thoughts and previous experiences. There are also solutions to common problems contained within the worksheet.

Step 2: Ask the client to complete worksheet 2, giving assistance and support where required.

Step 3: Transform the information on worksheet 2 into a CV! Either use one of the suggested styles from worksheet 3, or the client's own ideas, or a combination of both.

Step 4: Review the completed CV *from the employer's point of view.* Ask the following questions of the client, whilst they are occupying the role of the potential employer:

- What are your first thoughts on receiving this CV?

Ideally the initial thoughts should be positive ones. It is not always important exactly which thoughts they are. A good CV will encourage the employer to put the CV in a 'yes' pile or at least at the top of the to-be-considered pile.

- Do you feel that the CV is easy to read? If not, why?

Most people scan read without even thinking about it – this generally involves looking at about every third word and allowing your brain to guess the rest. This is why spelling mistakes can be so hard to find in our own work as well! If a CV does not 'flow', scan reading becomes difficult and the reading becomes a chore. Look at which bits of the CV act as stops to the flow of reading and consider how they could be changed.

- Is there any other information that you require or would like to see? If yes, what information?

Employers will have a list of requirements for candidates to possess and this information needs to be readily available on the CV. This may include items such as required licences, experience or qualifications. Knowing what information an employer wants is a crucial part of the career research for any employee. This information is usually contained in the 'skills' or 'person specification' part of the job application form.

- If you asked this person to an interview, what other information or questions would you ask them?

Conversely to the point above, too much information can be as off-putting as too little. A CV should whet the appetite of the employer and make them want to meet the person. If the answer to this question is that there are no questions left to ask, then there may be too much information on the CV.

63

Exercise 6 – Worksheet 1: Big No Nos

What are your thoughts, feelings and experiences of the following in relation to CV's?

1) Spelling errors: it makes the person seem careless and disinterested in applying for the position. And tis jsut vrey anoyyin… Don't rely on spell check and make sure that the document is set to UK spelling not US as there are distinct differences in spellings. Also, don't use colloquialisms or abbreviated 'text' speak; unless it would be useful in the position, and relevant to the post.

2) Overly long CVs: keep it to a maximum of 2 pages unless there is an exceptional reason why it needs to be longer. A CV is a resumé of your life, not a biography.

3) Huge font: this just highlights the lack of information in the CV rather than disguises it. The answer is to find more to write about, extend the personal statement, or use A5 paper instead of A4.

4) Poor grammar and punctuation: check that the grammar you have used makes the sentence read the way it was intended. There is a big difference between 'time to eat children' and 'time to eat, children'. And as Groucho Marx said – 'today I shot an elephant in my pyjamas' (how did the elephant get into his pyjamas?).

5) Poor proofreading: don't forget to change the job you're looking for in the personal statement to the role you are actually applying for.

6) Over enthusiasm: don't put too much emphasis on qualifications which are irrelevant to the position, or out-of-date, or painfully list every qualification ever undertaken; that scouting camp badge is great but not likely to get you a position in a bank.

7) Bizarre font choices: the CV needs to be easy to read, only go for 'out there' fonts if it would display a relevant and useful skill for the position you are applying for. Wingdings is always a bad idea – □〰 ⊠♏•.

8) Lying: you will get caught out at some point, which may be just plain embarrassing (if you can't actually speak Spanish), or it may be illegal. Just don't do it – have confidence in who you actually are and that someone will want to employ you for that alone, without the Oscar and Nobel peace prize.

9) Don't use unrealistic blurb: you need to get the employer's attention but they don't want to feel that it is just a spiel that you are 'rolling out' for everyone in a 10 mile radius. Keep it relevant.

10) Forgetting contact details (or getting the details wrong): it is so easy to transpose digits; check, check and check again. If an employer is interested in you, they need to be able to contact you. They won't spend hours tracking you down, they'll just move to the next person in line.

Common problems with CVs

Have you experienced any of the following problems in relation to CV's? Here are some solutions!

1) **Fragmented work history**

- ✓ Take the emphasis off the dates

- ✓ Group agency work together under the agency name

- ✓ Concentrate on skills/qualifications/certificates/positions held including voluntary work

(See CV example for John Smith)

2) **Low skills**

- ✓ Pull out good personality traits

- ✓ Emphasise transferable skills

- ✓ List qualifications/education

- ✓ List voluntary work?

(see CV example for Kerry Jones)

3) **Few or only one previous position**

- ✓ Much the same as for low skill – build up the personality and promote positive work ethic

- ✓ Emphasise transferable skills

- ✓ List any voluntary work

(see CV example for Bob Blue)

4) **Applying for the first 'official' job**

- ✓ Make the CV into more of a 1 page advert

- ✓ Or write a covering letter with CV details instead

- ✓ Add any voluntary work

(see CV example for Daniel Cramer)

5) **Too much information or experience**

- ✓ Be specific to the role being applied for

- ✓ Keep the detail to the relevant areas and/or the most recent. O Levels can be abbreviated!

- ✓ Keep it to 2 pages

(see CV example for Mary Jane Jenkins)

Exercise 6 – Worksheet 2

Name:

Address:

Contact details (number/email):

Qualifications:

Relevant qualifications:

Key skills:

Relevant licences/training:

Vocational training:

Education history:

Secondary school -

College/university -

Adult learning facilities –

Career history:

Previous positions:

(include position title, role details (brief) and dates)

1.

2.

3.

4.

Why do you want this particular role?

What can you offer the employer?

What positive attributes do you have?

Now rewrite the answers to the above 3 questions as your personal profile:

Relevant personal information:

Exercise 6 – Worksheet 3

J O H N   S M I T H

12 High Street, Anytown, County. HP01 2BC
Tel: 01234 56***0   Mob: 07677 32***4

Personal Profile

An experienced and hardworking individual who is self-motivated and an excellent team member. A punctual, well-presented person with a variety of practiced skills to offer and committed to providing a high standard of work.

Looking for a position as a **HOD CARRIER.** Available for immediate start

Key Skills

- CSCS health and safety passport

- Experience as hod carrier

- Flexible to employer's needs

- Capable manual worker

- Good literacy and numeracy skills

Site Experience

Experienced at assisting tradesmen in their duties including bricklaying, plastering and carpentry. Duties have also included manual handling of materials, loading and unloading, as well as delivering materials to parts of the site as required. Maintenance of a clean, safe workplace and tools were an integral part of positions held.

Also experienced in laying of decking to customer requirements, including groundwork to prepare and landscaping of the surrounding area to complete.

Work experience

Site Operative   Recruitment Agency&Co.   2004-2005
Positions held included **hod carrier**, labourer, groundworker and painter/decorator

Hod Carrier   Blue Street Agency   2003-2004
Worked as a **hod carrier** on different projects including the renovation of Stoke Mandeville Hospital

Labourer   Workerman Agency   2001-2002
Duties involved acting as a bricklayer's assistant, carpenter's assistant and groundwork

Education and Training

Manual handling   2005

CSCS Health and Safety passport   2004

OCN Literacy and numeracy Level 2   2004

Educated at the Abbey Centre from 1998-2000, achieved a GCSE in woodwork

12 High Street, Anytown, County. HP01 2BC
Tel: 01234 56***0   Mob: 0**77 3216**

Kerry Jones

A personable, hardworking individual who is committed to achieving aims and objectives. An excellent team member who approaches challenges enthusiastically and completes tasks to a high standard.

Key Skills

- Reliable and punctual

- Experienced at customer service

- Willing to learn

- Literacy and numeracy to level 2

Work Experience

Cleaning operative Wash&Go Maids Aug 2003-present

- Visiting and cleaning customers' homes.

- Customer satisfaction is an integral part of this job.

- Appointments must be made to suit the client and punctually kept.

- Cleaning is completed to a high standard, taking care of customer possessions and respecting privacy.

Cashier Fast Foods R us Feb 2000-Aug 2003

- Responsible for customer service and carried out the customer complaints role.

- Maintenance of a clean workplace hygiene and food safety were essential duties.

- Cash handling was a major part of the position as well as staying calm and efficient during busy periods.

Chambermaid   The Grand Hotel   Sept 1998 – Feb 2000

- Self-organisation of resources and planning of work according to customer needs.

- Cleaning and tidying was required to be quick and efficient.

- Privacy of residents was respected at all times.

Education and Training

Training course - Health and Safety in the workplace   2004

GCSEs in Maths, home technology and RE (Education Secondary School)   1998

Personal Information

Full Clean driving licence

Bob Blue

2 High Street,
Anytown,
County.
HP01 2BC
Mob: 07677 *****4

A highly motivated and capable individual with a variety of skills and experience to offer. Excellent communicator, experience of supervising staff and the ability to work under pressure and deliver to set targets.

Now looking for the opportunity to use and further these skills in an environment that will offer a challenge and a sense of personal achievement.

Career highlights

Supervised the completion of a large contract that resulted in the expansion of the company and the opening of a new warehouse.

Was involved in the final stages of recruitment and training for new staff.

Worked with the team to ensure the company won the 'Investor in People' award and continued to hold this award for the past 4 years.

Key Skills

Current forklift licence – counterbalance and reach

Supervisory experience

Well organised and punctual

Committed to achieving aims and objectives

Career history

Warehouse manager   Goods In&Out co.   Aug 1991- Dec 2004

Joined the company as a trainee warehouse operative and was promoted to manager in 1999. Experienced in undertaking and supervising all areas of warehousing including picking and packing, loading and unloading and forklift use. Also experienced in staff management, rotas, discipline and budgeting.

Personal Information

I enjoy keeping fit through running and weight training

DANIEL CRAMER

3a WENDLE HOUSE, MANSION LANE, SOUTHCOURT, AYLESBURY, BUCKS, HP21 7RL
MOB: 07417 *** ***

A punctual and hardworking person with an abundance of experience in construction.
Now looking for a position as a **semi-skilled labourer.**
A team player who is reliable and has excellent communication skills and a wealth of practical abilities.
Would benefit your construction site with my skill, abilities and personality.

WORK HISTORY:

Worked for the family firm providing various construction tasks for customers:

- **Tarmacking**
- **Concreting**
- **Roofing**
  - Including - Tiling, felting and battening
- **Landscaping**
  - Including - Hard landscaping, gardening and patio laying
- **Home maintenance**
  - Providing and fitting new guttering and uPVC fascia boards
- **Customer service**
  - Sales service and after-sales care

PERSONAL DETAILS:

DOB: 30.03.1982

MARY JANE JENKINS

12 High Street, Anytown, County. AA1 2BC
Tel: 01234 567890   Mobile: 07767 013579   Email: contactme@gmail.co.uk

---

Personal Statement

I enjoy working in a busy team environment, whilst also performing well when working under my own initiative. I take a positive pro-active approach to the acquisition of new skills and adaptation towards changes in the working environment. Following a promotion in 2005, I achieved a GCSE in Biology in order to enhance my knowledge; understanding the commitment to my new role. Similarly, I have continually kept abreast of advancements in ICT and am proficient in a number of applications including Excel, PowerPoint, Word XP (and Vista), Lotus Notes, Outlook and Reference Manager.

I believe the combination of secretarial and administrative skills and corporate experience together with my personal qualities of determination, self-discipline and organisation displayed through my study would be successfully and beneficially applied to the position of Personal Assistant.

Career History

The Principle Partnership (Anytown, County.)   Mar 2008 – Present
PA to Senior Partner/Office Manager

VetAdmin Ltd (Anytown, County.)   Jan 2005 – Feb 2008
Technical Services Assistant reporting to International Technical Manager (promoted 2005)

Animal Health Ltd (Anytown, County.)   June 1985 – Dec 2004
Secretary to Technical Manager

Printers Ltd   (Anytown, County.)   Sept 1970 - May 1985
Secretary to Managing Director

Construction UK Ltd (Anytown, County.)   1968-1970
Junior Secretary in Construction Department

Vocational Responsibilities

PA – International Safety Consultants

- All administrative duties to Technical Director
- Diary Management
- Secretariat to the International Intumescent Fire Seals Association
- Ensuring all documentation is circulated and logged for International Standards Organisation and British Standards Institute
- Organise travel and overseas standards meetings

Technical Services Assistant – VetAdmin Ltd.

- Assist in preparing and finalising dossiers, clinical record forms for regulatory affairs and clinical trial data management
- Managing scientific reference materials and database
- Handling veterinary medical and sales enquiries
- Organising diary and travel, including arranging of overseas conferencing
- Minute taking (using shorthand) and ensuring distribution to relevant personnel
- Credit Control and wholesaler management

Education and Training

ICS Limited GCSE Biology (C)   2007

Town College of Further Education Secretarial Course   1966-1967
Royal College of Arts Typewriting, Stages I, II and III (Distinction), Shorthand, 80wpm & 100wpm, Speech Training, Stage I

County Secondary School   1966-1967

CSE's: English Grade 1, Typing Grade 2, Accounts Grade 3, Art Grade 3,

---

PERSONAL INFORMATION:

Full clean driving licence

Exercise 6 – Review

Name at least one thing that has been learned from this exercise.

Additional Notes:

Exercise 7 – Job Applications

Tutor Notes

This exercise looks at job applications. This is often the first contact that an employer will have with the potential employee and it needs to count. So an important message here, is not to rush it. A negative first impression takes a long time to shake, if you even get the chance.

The application may be a formal application, it may be the CV or it may even be a verbal enquiry.

Note: A signed application form constitutes a legal document and so it is illegal to lie on one. To do so risks prosecution for obtaining a pecuniary advantage by deception.

For offenders, this exercise links with exercise 9 on disclosure of convictions.

Step 1: Provide the client with the quiz on worksheet 1. *Do not* read through it *for* them (this exercise may have to be left out if the literacy skills of the client are such that they cannot manage this task alone). State that this is a timed test and they are to do it as quickly as possible. Using any clock or watch, start the client off.

Step 2: Depending on whether the client read through the worksheet first, and therefore only completed the first question, or whether they raced ahead - the practitioner needs to discuss with the client the importance of reading through job application forms (and CVs) first to make sure that they have a full understanding *before* they start filling the form in. This is a very simple way of preventing silly mistakes.

Step 3: Complete worksheet 2 with the client on 'what employers are looking for' on application forms. The client needs to have an idea at this stage of the type of career or position they are looking for, so that their answers can be specific.

Tip: If the client struggles, get them to role play the employer to look at the application process from the employer's perspective.

Step 4: Remind the client that handing a CV to a prospective employer is also acceptable and for any work application, of any kind, the client should always follow it up with a phone call or email. The feedback can be invaluable.

Exercise 7 – Worksheet 1

You have to complete this series of questions in the shortest time possible – Go!

1. Write your name here _____.

2. Draw a square in the top right hand corner of this piece of paper.

3. Answer the following sum:

$$4 + 2 - 1 \times 0 = \underline{\hspace{2cm}}$$

4. Circle your name.

5. Tap your left thigh with your right hand three times.

6. Doodle a picture of yourself at the foot of this page.

7. Fold this piece of paper in to a paper aeroplane, throw it, retrieve it and carry on with the questions.

8. Stand up and say the month of your birth.

9. Look at the clock and note the time in the box below:

10. Answer only question 1.

11. Lick the tip of your left index finger.

12. Write the name of your favourite film here:

_____

Exercise 7 – Worksheet 2

What are employers looking for in answers to job application form questions?

When answering the following questions, think about the position, role or career that you are aiming for.

Job description and person specification

These are just posh ways of saying 'what you have to do every day' and 'the skills we think you need to have to accomplish this job'. Therefore when the application form asks you what skills you think you have, make sure your answer contains the skills the employer has stated they are looking for…

Match the following tasks to a relevant skill:

Customer service	personable	approachable
Use of a till	numerate	prepared to learn
Physical tasks such as lifting	fit	
Being a keyholder	trustworthy	
Supervision of staff	organised	

Write a bullet point list of likely daily activities for your chosen role

-

-

-

-

What skills would an employer be looking for in order to accomplish these tasks?

The dreaded 'why do you want this position?' question.

Well, why *do* you want it? Think of what you would like to achieve through the job. What is it about this role that will get you out of bed on a cold, wet, dark Monday morning? Where can you see yourself taking the role? You need to be able to provide evidence that you know their specific company above all the other similar ones, and that you are motivated to use the skills you have to the company's benefit, as well as your own.

Think of some ideas and note them here:

_____

_____

_____

_____

Strengths and weaknesses

Most application forms will ask the person to evaluate themselves in this manner. It's not about finding fault but reflecting on weaker areas and crucially, what the person concerned plans to do about this.

Look in to the 'mirror' below at yourself and write down around the edge things that come to mind when you think about yourself.

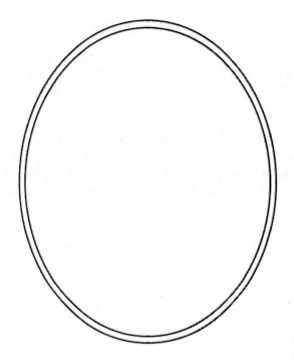

Sort the attributes you wrote above into two lists of positive and negative:

Positive	Negative	Revise the negatives here

What can you say about the negative ones that make them seem more of an advantage than disadvantage? For example, a slow typist could also be a careful one.

The final question – 'is there anything else you want to tell us?'

This question is about giving the person applying for the job a chance to shine and be unique, to stand out above the crowd. Think about all the preparation you have already done through this workbook. Is there any information that the application form has not asked you for?

Always follow up any application or contact with a prospective employer with a phone call or email. This is not to harass them into employing you but to ask for feedback. Ask what they thought of your application, how could you improve it, and what additional skills or traits are they looking for? Then use this feedback to inform your next application!

Exercise 7 – Review

Name at least one thing that has been learned from this exercise.

Additional Notes:

Exercise 8 – Interviews

Tutor Notes

Some people find that the scariest part of seeking a job is the job interview. However, it is often the essential part that enables an employer to make up their mind about someone.

This exercise ends with a role play with the client playing both the employer and the prospective employee. The idea is that if the interviewee is able to understand things from the employer's perspective, they will understand more as to what the employer is looking for.

The practitioner may need to do some research into the client's applied-for position in order to provide a realistic interview scenario.

Step 1: Ask the client to draw a scruffy dressed person and then a tidily dressed person in the boxes on worksheet 1. Ask the client to note (or state) what they think when they first see the two people if *they were an employer*. Do they think the people would benefit the employer's business and represent the image they are looking for? Note the client's ideas around the edge of the relevant picture.

Note: this exercise is not about being judgemental, it's about being realistic and how, when meeting someone for the first time, first impressions count. Especially, if one person wants something from the other – like a job!

Step 2: Thinking about the position/career that the client would like, ask them to write (or sketch) on the blank person in worksheet 1 what clothing and accessories (including the level of jewellery and perfume/aftershave) they think would be appropriate. Also include things to leave out. There is no point gassing out the interview panel with a favoured scent or turning up with lots of jewellery for a position in a butchers' shop.

Step 3: The last section on worksheet 1 is about the client's 'nervous signs'; being aware of these signs assists the client in managing them so that a calm image is presented at interview.

Step 4: Worksheet 2 contains some questions that may be asked at interview. Ask the client to read the question and consider what is actually being asked. Support this as appropriate but do not *tell* the offender what the answer is (remember MI (see section one) – nobody wants advice).

For example, with the question 'tell me about yourself', the employer is not asking for the client's takeaway preference... they are asking the client to reiterate the skills and attributes they possess which makes them suitable for the position and which will benefit the company.

Tip: The following steps require some preparation from the practitioner. The room needs to be arranged as it may be in an interview (interviewer facing the interviewee, possibly across a desk or table). Don't be afraid to go the whole hog, if it will benefit the client, and role play from when they enter your building.

Step 5: This step may be better run as a separate session. Ask the client to imagine themselves as the employer for their chosen career. The facilitator will play the interviewee at this point. The client needs to think of five questions to ask and note them on worksheet 3. As the interview progresses, they need to complete the sections on worksheet 3. Depending on the facilitator's knowledge of the client, they can choose to be a perfect candidate, a struggling one, or a so-so one.

Tip: If the client struggles with literacy, it may be that another practitioner is needed to provide support at this stage. However, the client needs to feel comfortable doing a role play in front of the third person.

Step 6: Go through worksheet 3 with the client after the role play. Look at the points they have noted and how they may apply to the client's interview technique.

Step 7: Swap places and allow the client to role play the interviewee, to the best of their ability. The practitioner needs to provide constructive feedback at the end of this.

Step 8: Worksheet 4 is simply a checklist for the client to have which they can use prior to any interview. Detach this from the workbook and let them take it away.

Exercise 8 – Worksheet 1

Draw a picture of a scruffy looking person in the box below:	Draw a picture of a smartly dressed person in the box below:

Write or draw what clothing and accessories are appropriate for your interview.

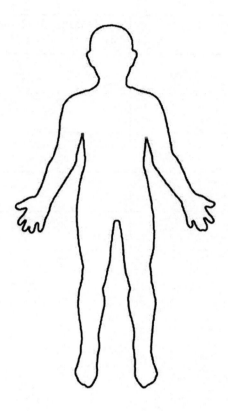

Any definite no nos?

-
-
-
-
-

What signs do you give off that you are nervous or fidgety?

Sign	How can you address this?
e.g. Twiddling with my hair	e.g. Holding my hands together in my lap

Exercise 8 – Worksheet 2

In an interview situation, what are these questions actually asking?

Tell me about yourself?

Give an example of an answer you could use.

Why should we employ you over the other candidates?

Give an example of an answer you could use.

Name a strength and a weakness of yours.

Give an example of an answer you could use.

Why are you changing jobs/roles?

Give an example of an answer you could use.

Where do you see yourself in five years' time?

Give an example of an answer you could use.

How would you handle a dispute between yourself and another colleague?

Give an example of an answer you could use.

And slightly stranger questions.

Name three items you would take with you on a long journey?

Give an example of an answer you could use.

What inspirational characters, dead or alive, fictitious or real, would you invite to a dinner party?

Give an example of an answer you could use.

Exercise 8 – Worksheet 3

Note your first impression of the candidate.

Are they smartly dressed? Did they present themselves well? Were they polite? Do they look like they wanted to be here?

Note your five questions:

Question 1...

How do you rate the interviewee's answer?

Question 2...

How do you rate the interviewee's answer?

Question 3...

How do you rate the interviewee's answer?

Question 4...

How do you rate the interviewee's answer?

Question 5...

How do you rate the interviewee's answer?

Would you like to employ this person?

Give reasons for your answer:

Exercise 8 – Worksheet 4

Interview checklist

Have you researched the company?

What is their main trade/who are their main trading partners?

Where is the head office?

What are the career prospects like?

How big is the company/how many staff?

What is the main product?

What will your main responsibilities be?

How are you getting to the interview?

Do you know the bus/train timetable?

Do you have money for the bus/train fare?

Do you know where the nearest car park is?

Do you have money for the car park?

Do you have the number for the office in case you are running late?

What do you need to take with you? (some employers will ask for evidence of ID, right to work documents, and so on)

What is the appropriate clothing?

Are you likely to have to demonstrate any practical skills?

Do you need to take any tools of your trade?

Exercise 8 – Review

Name at least one thing that has been learned from this exercise.

Additional Notes:

Exercise 9 – Disclosure of Convictions

Tutor Notes

This exercise starts with a note of caution that the practitioner must understand – disclosure of convictions is a legal matter. If the client gets it wrong, it could potentially lead to a further conviction. Note the following:

1. It is illegal for a client to lie, omit, falsify or change convictions when asked; 'asking' can include job application forms, verbally, and on contracts.

2. A person does not have to disclose their convictions unless asked.

3. It is illegal to apply for a position that a client knows they are barred from holding (for example, being on the barred list for working with children and applying for a teaching assistant post).

4. Ignorance is never accepted as an excuse; a person cannot state in their defence that they were unaware of the law. It is their responsibility to find out.

If, at any stage, there are any areas which the practitioner or offender is unsure about, contact another organisation, such as NACRO, for support.

The practitioner needs to support the offender in understanding that disclosing offences is not necessarily the end game for a job application. If an employer rejects the client solely on their offending history (quite apart from being illegal, unless the conviction is relevant to the post) the offender needs to ask themselves whether they would want to work for an employer like that...
It may have been a near miss for them, for a position they would have been miserable in. It is harder to get a job with convictions and there is no point in being gentle about that fact - but the crucial point is that it is possible.

Information sheet 1 is replicated from section one for easy reference for the practitioner.

Information sheet 2 is the 'where, when, how' of disclosure.

Step 1: Complete the chart on worksheet 1 with the offender so that they are aware which of their convictions are spent and unspent. Be careful to note any convictions made at Crown Court as this impacts on other convictions which were unspent at the time of sentencing at Crown Court.

Step 2: Make sure that the offender is fully aware of the caveats attached to the Rehabilitation of Offenders Act 1974, especially that some positions are 'exempt' from the Act and therefore the concept of spent convictions does not apply.

Note: Once disclosed, the information regarding a person's convictions is privileged information and the employer is under a legal obligation **not** to disseminate it to a wider group of people than necessary. Reassure the client that the employer will not be able to gossip about them or their convictions.

Step 3: The practitioner needs to facilitate an open and honest discussion regarding the pros and cons of disclosing convictions. Whilst an obvious downside to non-disclosure is the illegality of this, it would be imprudent of the practitioner to assume that this is sufficient to put a client off hiding their convictions. During this part of the exercise, the practitioner needs to discuss each point raised with the offender in more depth, not just list the points on worksheet 2.

Step 4: The offender needs then to write their own disclosure statement. Worksheet 3 is a prompt sheet and a structure to base their statement around. The key points for the facilitator are that the statement must indicate that the offender:

- takes responsibility for their offence(s) in full and does not attempt to blame others
- demonstrates remorse for the offence(s)
- can evidence/explain what they have done since the offence to ensure that a repeat of the offending behaviour does not happen again

Step 5: Discuss information sheet 2 with the offender, with specific reference to their chosen career. If appropriate, this sheet can be referred to again when the client applies for a position and needs to decide on the how/where/when of disclosure.

Exercise 9 – Information Sheet 1

Conviction	Rehabilitation period (if 17 or under when convicted)	Rehabilitation period (if 18 or over when convicted)
Prison sentence of 6 months or less	3.5 years	7 years
Prison sentence of over 6 months but not exceeding 2.5 years (30 months)	5 years	10 years
Borstal	7 years	7 years
Detention Centre	3 years	3 years
Fines, compensation order, action plan and reparation orders	2.5 years	5 years
Probation order, community service, combination order, drug treatment and testing order (DTTO) (prior to Feb 95) Community Rehabilitation Order (CRO), Community Punishment Order (CPO), Community Rehabilitation and Punishment Order (CPRO) (from Feb 95 to Apr 05) Community Orders with Requirements (from Apr 05)	2.5 years	5 years
Absolute Discharge	6 months	6 months
Detention and Training Order of less than 6 months	1 year after the order expires	3.5 years
Detention and Training Order of more than 6 months	1 years after the order expires	5 years
Hospital Order	The longest period of: 5 years or 2 years after the order expires	
Referral Order	Once the order expires	

Note that it is the *sentence* which is relevant to the rehabilitation period *not* the *offence* itself.

Caution: It is a criminal offence to fail to disclose relevant convictions when asked. Therefore, if the practitioner is in any way unsure about the application of this Act to their client, they *must* seek help from a more knowledgeable source.

The rehabilitation period is the time until the conviction is 'spent'. Spent convictions do not usually have to be disclosed.

If an offender reoffends whilst the rehabilitation period of a previous offence is still current, this needs to be taken into account *if* the new offence is one that is tried in a Crown Court. Any offences which remain unspent at the time of the new Crown Court offence will fall under the new rehabilitation period for the new offence. Therefore, it is possible that a client may have a list of minor, summary, offences which will never become spent as they were unspent at the time when that client was convicted for a new offence, and sentenced to over two and a half years in prison.

For example:

In 2000, Brian is convicted of theft and sentenced to a Community Rehabilitation Order or CRO. The rehabilitation period for this is five years and so this offence will be spent in 2005.

However, in 2003, Brian is convicted of Grievous Bodily Harm (GBH) and sentenced to three years imprisonment. Such a sentence means that this conviction will never be considered as 'spent'.

At the time of the conviction for GBH, the rehabilitation period for the theft was still active (the offence was 'unspent') and as such, the theft now comes under the rehabilitation period for the new offence. Therefore, neither offence will ever be spent.

If an offender is sentenced to consecutive prison terms, the total time is the figure to be considered in order to work out the rehabilitation period. However, if the terms are concurrent, then the terms only need to be considered separately.

There will be times when an application forms states that the position being applied for is '*exempt from the Rehabilitation of Offenders Act 1974*'. If this is the case, then it must be made clear on the application form. Instances where this may occur include, but are not limited to, positions which involve working with children or vulnerable adults and those which involve national security. In this event, *all* convictions must be disclosed – even those that would in other circumstances be considered as spent.

Exercise 9 – Information Sheet 2

There are different points during a job application where an offender may choose to disclose their convictions. The choice is dependent on the offender's confidence (it takes a lot to disclose convictions face-to-face with a potential employer), the type of position, and the style of job application. It is not a defence, subsequently, for an offender to say that they had 'no opportunity' to disclose, although legally no-one has to disclose unless asked (unless they are aware they have a relevant conviction which they *must* disclose or are on a barred list). However, if they are not asked, the offender still needs to ask themselves whether they would like to work for a company without providing disclosure - should a later admission (or discovery of the convictions) cause difficulties. Sometimes, starting on a clean sheet is better.

The 'how' of disclosure is covered in step 4 of worksheet 3; a prepared disclosure statement is recommended as it allows the client to rehearse what it is they want to get across to the employer.

The following addresses the opportunities to disclose convictions in the likely order the opportunity will arise; it is not in the 'best' order to disclose.

CV

Whilst it would be possible to put convictions on a CV, especially to explain long gaps, it is not generally recommended. A person's convictions are privileged information and a CV is designed to be sent out everywhere in bulk, therefore more people than necessary would end up knowing about the convictions.

Job application form

Most official job application forms ask whether the applicant has any unspent convictions. Any position which is exempt from the ROA '74 will state this fact at this point and ask for all convictions to be disclosed. As the client will sign the job application form, and therefore turn it into a legal document, it is an offence to lie on this form. However, it can be very difficult to feel able to list or state all convictions on a form, without the opportunity to explain the circumstances or what positive things have been done since. Therefore, two suggestions to reach a middle ground are:

- To write 'to be disclosed at interview' where the form asks for the convictions. This counts as disclosing that the person has convictions but means that there is an opportunity to discuss it more in-depth, with the appropriate people, at a later date. It also has the added benefit of inviting oneself to an interview!

- To enclose the completed disclosure statement in a sealed envelope, addressed 'to whom it may concern' and clearly marked 'confidential'. This may be the better approach for those who do not feel confident enough to disclose for the first time in interview. Even with this approach, a candidate is still likely to be asked to discuss matters in the interview though.

At interview

If the offender has indicated previously that they have a conviction, the subject is likely to arise in the interview. The client needs to be prepared for this and think/practice how to discuss it. Consider what questions the employer is likely to ask. As a foundation, an employer could be expected to want to know:

- What the offence actually was (most conviction titles tell people very little about what the person actually *did*). An offender should be careful here not to try and absolve themself of responsibility for the offence...
- When the offence occurred.
- What the impact on the company may be from employing a person with that conviction, both in terms of publicity and for the other staff members.
- What has that person done since to make sure that the circumstances which led to the offence do not occur again.

If the subject is not raised in the interview but the offender wishes to provide disclosure, most interviews close with the question of 'do you have anything you want to add or ask?', or something similar. This can be used as an opportunity to disclose. There are obvious downsides to spending all the interview convincing employers that a client is the perfect candidate and then potentially blindsiding them with the disclosure. Sometimes it is difficult to plan the exact moment, it may be better to have the actual disclosure statement prepared and be more fluid with the 'when'.

It is acceptable to take the written disclosure statement to an interview and either use it as a prompt sheet or ask the employer to read it in their presence.

After interview

Due to the personal nature of conviction disclosure and the high likelihood that employers will want to ask questions, disclosing after the interview has finished has inherent problems. It is possible to phone the company at a later date and disclose but the face-to-face opportunity has been lost. Also, employers may feel duped by the fact that the candidate did not disclose at interview – this is not a positive feeling for a prospective employer to have. However, if the client chooses to do this, they could disclose their convictions via a letter addressed specifically to the person who interviewed them, or they could phone the person concerned or the HR department (if the company is large enough to have one). Alternatively, they could try to arrange another meeting.

Following appointment to the position

Again this is not recommended but the situation may occur if the offender has chosen not to disclose and has not been asked but the employment contract they now need to sign states that all convictions must be disclosed. A signed contract is a legal document so to sign it and still not provide disclosure would be illegal. The methods of disclosure at this point would be similar to the ones suggested above.

During employment

As stated above, most contracts will state that convictions need to be disclosed. The difficulty with disclosing at this point is that, even where there was no illegality in the lack of previous disclosure, the employer may not look favourably on an employee if they feel they were lied to, or that important information had been withheld from them. However, disclosing at this stage does mean that the offender has had the opportunity to prove themselves as an employee, which may work in their favour.

Note: whichever method the client chooses, they must be confident that they are acting legally.

Exercise 9 – Worksheet 1

Complete the worksheet by writing out offences in date order (from the date convicted as this is the date the rehabilitation period runs from, not the date the offence was committed). Use the table on information sheet 1 to help.

Conviction (offence)	Sentence	Date spent

If, once the table is completed, the date the offences become spent do not run in date order (due to the different types of sentences), it may be helpful to rewrite the table in date order for the last column.

IT IS A CRIMINAL OFFENCE TO FAIL TO DISCLOSE RELEVANT CONVICTIONS. DO NOT GUESS – BE SURE.

Exercise 9 – Worksheet 2

Complete, through discussion, the following table into the benefits and disadvantages of disclosing convictions to a potential employer.

Pros	Cons

Exercise 9 – Worksheet 3

The disclosure statement

Before you start:

1. Think about what you are trying to achieve here – an employer is not a court, the police or your friend; consequently they are not interested in rehashing the case in detail, hearing about how it was a 'fit up', or exaggerations of any form.
2. The legal part of this statement is the actual disclosure, beyond that you are free to say what you want. You need to convince an employer that you have taken responsibility for the offence, taken the necessary lessons on board, and moved on.
3. The most important part of this statement will be the bits about *why* you will make a good employee.
4. Work through the next set of questions, then turn the answers into a statement. An example is given at the end. Not all of the questions will be relevant; each statement needs to be adjusted to suit the owner and the job. If you have more than one conviction, simply talk about the offences in the plural.

What is your conviction for, when were you sentenced, and what were you sentenced to?

Briefly describe the offence and explain why it happened (if you have more than one conviction, talk about them as a group).

How do you feel about the offence(s) now?

What have you done, or put in place, to ensure that you do not reoffend?

Why would you make a good employee?

Example statement for one offence:

I was convicted of common assault in August 2010 and sentenced to 200 hours Unpaid Work which I completed in February 2011, having requested additional hours per week to the minimum required.

The offence occurred whilst I was out drinking with friends and I entered into a fight. At the time I felt that I was defending a friend but I now realise that my actions were aggressive and caused harm to the victim.

I am very sorry for the harm that I caused and would not behave in such a manner again.

Since my conviction, I have sought advice from an alcohol agency and reduced my drinking to within the government guidelines. I also choose to socialise with different friends. Further, I have returned to college and completed a level 2 literacy qualification.

I believe that my skills are well suited to the position for which I have applied; I have the experience necessary and am a hardworking and thorough employee. I understand that I will have to work hard to prove myself but I am prepared to do this, which can only benefit the company.

Example statement for several offences:

I have three convictions for theft and one for possession of cannabis, dating from November 2004 to April 2008. My last conviction resulted in a sentence of supervision which I completed in April 2009. My offences occurred during a time when I was struggling financially and I made some poor decisions in order to manage this. I now realise the harm that I caused through my offending and I regret that I chose to behave the way I did.

During my last supervision, I worked with my Probation Officer to address the underlying issues which led to my offending, including poor budgeting skills and I feel that I have improved in every area. I am looking to continue my good progress and have made plans to manage any difficult circumstances, should they arise again. I am happy to discuss this further, if you have any questions.

I am confident that I will be able to fulfil the duties of this position to their fullest extent and I look forward to meeting and overcoming the challenges as they arise. I believe that my experiences have given me an edge when it comes to confronting and rising above adversity, and I feel that this ability can only benefit the company.

Exercise 9 – Review

Name at least one thing that has been learned from this exercise.

Additional Notes:

Exercise 10 – Managing Rejection

> **Tutor Notes**
>
> Whilst it would be nice to think that the client will gain employment from their first interview, the more likely scenario is that they may have to undertake several interviews before they are successful.
>
> If the client is getting interviews and not being successful, then the client may feel they have 'failed' given the amount of preparation, especially if they have completed this workbook, they will have put into the preparation stage.
>
> This exercise aims to help the client put each interview into perspective and use their experience as a learning curve to make sure that they do finally get the position they want. It is worth reminding the client that for each interview and position available, there will be more people that aren't 'successful' than are.

Prior to a job interview or application, it is likely that the possibility of not being successful is not given a second thought. Generally, we do not prepare to fail as this would be counter-intuitive. However, not getting exactly what we want is part of life and being able to deal with this is essential. Taking the step to ask for feedback is also important and so often forgotten.

Step 1: With the client, discuss the interview they attended. Ask them to describe the non-threatening parts first (such as the room, the people present or even the coffee laid on) and then move onto the actual interview. Use the worksheet as a prompt.

Tip: Acknowledge with the client that their feelings of being hard-done-by, and let down after all their preparation, are okay and part of the process.

Step 2: Assist the client in ordering their thoughts so that they make sense and are useful for the next job application or interview. Again, use the worksheet where appropriate.

Step 3: Cut out and allow the client to keep the card at the end of the worksheet.

Tip: If your client is not a visual learner, try adapting the exercise by role playing any important parts of the interview with them. Allow the client to play the interviewer so that they can then give themselves constructive feedback (you will need to have taken notes in step 1 for information).

Another alternative would be to blow up several balloons. Make notes on each of the balloons (one point for each balloon) of either issues or positive bits of the interview as the client recounts the experience in step 1. Ask the client to sort the balloons into positive and negative points. Allow the client to 'pop' the negative balloons as they come up with a positive alternative for it.

Exercise 10 – Worksheet 1

- Were you on time?

- Did you find the address okay?

- What was the building like? How friendly were the staff and others there?

- What were the interviewers like?

- Describe the process of the interview (Was it all talking? Were there any exercises? Any bizarre questions?)

- What went well?

- What didn't go so well?

- Any thoughts since? What are you thinking 'I wish had just…' about?

- Why do you feel so rubbish about not getting this *particular* position?

- What can you take forwards from the experience?

- Have you asked for feedback? If not, why not?! (how else do we learn…?)

List the five biggest negatives you can think of from the experience:

1

2

3

4

5

Now, look at those negatives from another viewpoint and make each negative a positive point to learn from and do differently. For example, if a negative was that you felt you didn't answer the questions fully enough, the point to take forwards would be to either have notes or to research the company more fully next time.

1

2

3

4

5

Keep this card throughout your career hunting experience:

> **Don't take it personally**
> It wasn't a judgement on you as a person – you are more than just your qualifications and experience.
>
> **Learn from the experience**
> Ask for feedback and listen to the answers – incorporate them into your next interview or application.
>
> **Look forward to the next chance**
> What doesn't kill us makes us stronger – there will be the perfect opportunity for you out there; go and find it.

Exercise 10 – Review

Name at least one thing that has been learned from this exercise.

Additional Notes:

Exercise 11 – The Final Review

Tutor Notes

This session is a motivational exercise aimed at empowering the client by emphasising what they have taken from the work you have conducted with them to date. It is worth noting here that when undertaking this exercise it should be facilitated so that it is in-keeping with the principles of Motivational Interviewing. Therefore, do not *tell* the client what they have taken from the session, rather simply summarise (or ask them to recall) the sessions you did with them, and ask them what they have taken from the sessions.

Note: Although this session is simple - try not to rush it.

Step 1: Ask the client to try and summarise what they have learned from completing this workbook. Use the titles of the exercises as a prompt if required. Also, ask the client to review the goals they set in exercise 4 and where appropriate, reset and progress them. List the answers on worksheet 1.

Step 2: Ask the client to list five reasons why they will succeed in gaining the position they want and five things that this success will bring them. Write these on worksheet 2 and allow the client to keep the worksheet at the end of the session.

Step 3: Congratulate the client for completing the work you have gone through and review the sessions when needed in the future.

Exercise 11 – Worksheet 1

Write down what you have learned from the exercises in this workbook.

1.

2.

3.

4.

5.

6.

7.

8.

9.

10.

Exercise 11 – Worksheet 2

5 reasons I will succeed
1.
2.
3.
4.
5.

5 positive things I will gain from my success
1.
2.
3.
4.
5.

Cut out and keep.

Good luck ☺

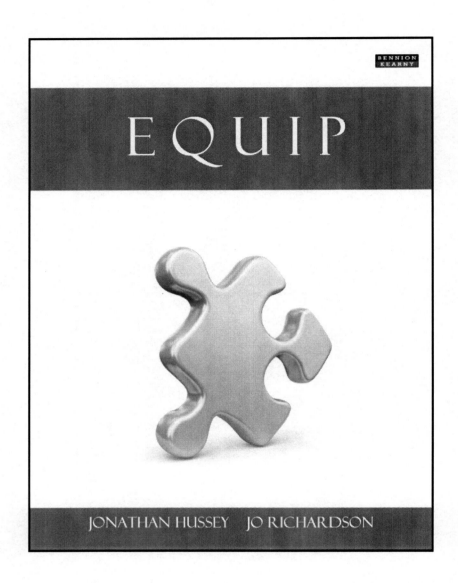

This workbook has been developed in conjunction with EQUIP -
a resource for the client to use and keep, on their path to employment. EQUIP
can also be used as a standalone workbook for the more motivated
and able client to complete on their own.

ISBN: 978-0-9570511-7-1

See http://www.bennionkearny.com/Probation-Workbooks.htm for more details

Lightning Source UK Ltd.
Milton Keynes UK
UKOW02f1809101013

218868UK00010B/421/P